STRAW IN THE SUN

STRAW IN THE SUN

A Memoir

CHARLIE MAY SIMON
Edited by Aleshia O'Neal

THE UNIVERSITY *of* ARKANSAS PRESS

Fayetteville

2025

ISBN: 978-1-68226-266-5
eISBN: 978-1-61075-831-4

29 28 27 26 25 5 4 3 2 1

Manufactured in the United States of America

Designed by William Clift

♾ The paper used in this publication meets the minimum requirements of the American National Standard for Permanence of Paper for Printed Library Materials Z39.48-1984.

Cataloging-in-Publication Data on file at the Library of Congress.

Straw in the Sun

I am startled that God can make me so rich even with my own cheap stores. It needs but a few wisps of straw in the sun, some small word dropped, or that has lain long silent in some book. —THOREAU

Contents

Introduction

FOR those of us who rely on technology to provide information with just a swipe or a click, it can be hard to grasp the impact the printed word once had before the arrival of modern electronic devices. Yet imagine what it must have been like, as a young reader in rural America during the 1930s and '40s, to find a voice in children's literature like Charlie May Simon's, a voice that seemed to understand the life that surrounded you. Instead of stories of cities and adventures beyond your experience or imagination, the author spoke of simple subsistence living in the Ozark hills, the plight of sharecroppers in the Arkansas Delta, or life on a riverboat on the White River. 1930s Arkansas—the setting for many of Simon's stories for children, as well as for her 1945 memoir *Straw in the Sun*—held little advance of modernity: farming was still largely nonmechanized, while the prosperity of the state was intricately linked to agricultural production. Society was both racially and economically divided. For children growing up in this era, life was often a struggle in scarcity; it was the Great Depression, and times were hard.

Speaking in poetic prose about characters who were fully developed and growing through hardship while remaining optimistic, the author planted seeds of hope and perseverance in the lives of children across the nation. Simon's young readers were taught through the example of heroic yet ordinary characters—characters who looked a lot like them—that life had the potential for happiness and success despite present circumstances. These readers grew to expect a new adventure from Simon annually, as they looked forward to meeting her new characters and learning life lessons vicariously through their experiences. As they turned the pages, they were gratified to find stories where an attitude of acceptance prevailed over socioeconomic judgment, and where understanding confronted prejudice.

Two other Arkansas authors, Margaret Jones Bolsterli in *Born in the Delta: Reflections on the Making of a Southern White Sensibility* (1991) and John Grisham in *A Painted House* (2001), refer to painted houses as an example of status during the Depression. The grey, weathered houses whose occupants could not afford the luxury of paint represented the lower-rung social classes reserved for hill people, sharecroppers, and others of poor socioeconomic standing. Yet in Simon's novels, social stigmas were challenged, viewed from the perspective of the marginalized; the unpainted houses were entered, instead of their occupants remaining ignored or even excluded. Children living in those houses, therefore, found a nonjudgmental friend when they encountered Simon's books at the library. At the same time, children who lived in painted houses were given an opportunity to explore and question their systemic prejudices, also through the pen of a nonjudgmental friend who gently pushed for awareness. This is the literary legacy of Charlie May Simon, an Arkansas author who, over a writing career that spanned more than four decades, produced twenty-nine books for children, young adults, and adults.

* * *

The importance of community is a prominent theme throughout Simon's writings, including *Straw in the Sun,* where the
author describes community life during her homestead years.
Specifically in this memoir, Simon addresses the hill people
she lived among and their culture of community in four ways:
1) how those who are considered outsiders are not allowed to
participate within the community; 2) how the community
functions in a time of crisis; 3) how the community deals justice for crimes committed within its borders; and 4) how the
community sustains the members within its circle.

Community and Nature Barring Outsiders

In early spring of 1931, Simon and her husband, artist Howard
Simon, traveled from New York City to Perry County,
Arkansas, to homestead on thirty acres near Cove Creek.[1]
Simon gathered her recollections of this experience in *Straw
in the Sun,* published a decade after she left her cabin on
homestead land. As she opens the story, the author relates
how she had once "been part of this landscape. Its life and
mine were one" (5). In this statement, Simon reveals the status
she achieved during her homestead years: she was an integral
part of the community, a part of the lives of her neighbors
who saw the hills of Perry County as home, a part of the land
to which she had retreated. Yet, time did not stand still; life
did not wait for her return in order to continue. It moved
on without her. In her absence, the forest closed protectively
over the gap where she had created a temporary dwelling in
a culture that fought to preserve its own existence. She had
not come to stay, and the gap did not remain either.

Charlie May Simon's cabin in Perry County, Arkansas. *John Gould Fletcher / Charlie May Simon photograph collection, PHO.32, Box 2, Folders 84 and 85, Butler Center for Arkansas Studies, Roberts Library Central Arkansas Library System.*

What Simon left behind was a belonging, to both a culture and the land. Revisiting the spot where her cabin once stood, she is "like a ghost returning to a place once loved" (3). While she is observing the ruts in the road where their tires traveled, we see her mind is like the path. Nostalgia for the past meets reality of the present. In this haunting introduction, we see what is revealed to Simon upon her return, nearly a decade after her departure. Instead of a vibrant life, which she felt she would have upon leaving the homestead, she is reliving her memories nostalgically. She is describing a fallen world, a garden of Eden from which she has been barred. Instead of angels with flaming swords standing guard to prevent entrance, her banishment exists in the charred ruins of her cabin—a cabin built with the hands of her neighbors to allow Simon admission to their community. The burning of the homestead cabin is the act that removes the portal through which she could journey back into time, to recreate the memories and share them with her new husband, who has not participated in the rituals that led to her acceptance in this hill community. She is now an outsider; the door to the community is shut.

Through the flashback of an innocent child, concluded at the memoir's end, information is relayed to Simon and her new husband, John Gould Fletcher: you are outsiders, but I'll share our stories, our heritage. By retelling the community's shared story, the young orator realizes who Simon is. His method is a test that reveals her hidden identity, which her new clothes, new husband, and new life masked at first glance. Yet the young man states when her flashback is complete, "I know who you are, now. I could see it when I talked about your house burning" (243). Although the message is conveyed through a story within a story, its meaning is clear: memories and oral traditions of storytelling remain a constant in the hill culture she left behind. And they remain a constant in her own life; as a litmus test, the young man touches her own storyteller's heart, revealing what lies hidden in its depths. She had been one with the land and the people who lived there, and she longs to return to those days of simplicity.

But Simon is now like the "ghost neighbor," whose abandoned homestead she visits throughout her time at Rocky
Crossing. Simon transplants flowers that Mrs. Lewis loved
yet left behind, and her sense of this ghost neighbor is
deeply entwined with her thoughts about the wilderness
shutting out those who leave. This reinforces the feeling
she relates in the memoir's introduction: that the wilderness community closes the gap to protect itself. Simon
knows instinctively that the way is barred, stating, "The
wilderness has a way of drawing a curtain over itself to
shut out all who leave it, and to enclose all who had come
here" (48).

Nonetheless, the author recognizes that self-sufficiency
is an essential advantage of living in a remote community
that sustains itself, in part, by alienating outsiders. In her
memoir, we see her pride at the accomplishment of self-
sufficiency on the homestead:

> My house was never quite complete. There were always
> things to dream of adding some day: a screen porch, more
> closets and perhaps even plumbing at some far-off time. But
> it was home to me, the home I had always wanted, and it
> was made of the things of the earth, of trees and stones and
> the labor of my neighbors. All I needed to buy from town
> were nails, windowpanes and screens, cement, and oil and
> turpentine and powdered colors to mix the stain. The lum
> ber for the floors and sills and ceiling was sawed at a lum
> ber mill, not many miles away. Now I was standing on my
> own land, with a home of my own, and the only price I had
> to pay was work with my hands and less than five hundred
> dollars in money. (16)

Charlie May Simon pictured at the homestead site after her cabin was burned.
Series II, Box 5, 351, Charlie May Simon Papers, 1390-1977, UALR.MS.0006.

Contentment is what causes the house to remain uncompleted. Simon claims she would seek to improve the house with modern conveniences in the future. Yet, the house becomes a home when children and gatherings with neighbors are welcomed into the structure; only then does it contain and sustain life, allowing her an open door to participate in the community.

Community in Times of Crisis

Exploring the concept of community during crisis, Simon relays the death of the Massery baby. In this experience, she learns traditions that rule her neighbors' lives, tales of superstition that bind them together, and societal structures that are placed upon them. Simon learns that women do not gather with the men but stay in their societal place with other women. To be accepted, she has to adapt to their social customs.

In this community event, stark reality contradicts what is generally perceived as hope and life: the birth of a child. In the case of the Massery family, death replaces life, and despair in surroundings replaces hope. Simon recounts this scene also to show her purpose in redeeming the child Vannie, who will come to live with her; she chooses to impact the young girl's life to redeem the life that was lost. Her attention is not on the death, but on the life in front of her and the difference she can make in the life of the dead child's sibling.

As she leaves the community burial, Simon is given the gift of the hen and chicks that will appear in her recurring nightmare. To Simon, this offering signals a rite of passage; her acceptance of the community's ritual ways in the death of a child allows her admission to the community. She is now an insider. The hen and chicks are a gift of acceptance in return, as she is learning to be a part of the culture of rural Perry County. Perhaps her nightmare, which begins to recur after her departure from the homestead, symbolizes her guilt over leaving her neighbors' hospitality and all that had bound them together in experiencing life and death as a community.

Another example of community in times of crisis occurs in Simon's first winter at Rocky Crossing. She discovers she has lost her money when the bank holding all her savings fails. After Uncle George spreads the word through the community grapevine, folks rally around her, providing for her during this time of need: "News spreads fast in an isolated settlement where there are no newspapers. The story was told of my loss when the bank failed, and the amount grew with each telling. Then it was that I learned it is the poor who are the more generous, and who offer their friendship more readily" (29). As a result of losing the financial stability her savings provided, both of Simon's feet are now firmly planted in the homesteading life—her land. She becomes one with nature and with her "ghost neighbor," finding a sacred place of memory in this neighbor's abandoned homestead.

A transformation then occurs: in Simon's new life without modern conveniences or money, she embraces poverty in exchange for richness in nature. She experiences this metamorphosis in her own life as well as in nature, as spring comes to Rocky Crossing. As a result of leaving behind modernity and the possibility of returning to her previous life, she begins to become one with the land and community:

Something went wrong with the clutch band of the automobile, and there was no mechanic for thirty-five miles. Then the battery died from lack of use. The automobile stood in the yard, a useless piece of machinery. It was just as well, for there was no money to buy gasoline to run it. My old life was behind me now, and I became aware of the new. I was closer to the foxes that had their den near the hollow sycamore and the deer that came to the narrows for the salty taste of the earth there.

I began to notice things I had not seen before. . . . It was like sitting in a darkened theater, waiting for the play to begin. The orchestra marches in, the fiddles begin to tune, and you sit waiting, with a thrill of expectancy. At last the lights go out, the curtain slowly rises, and the play is on (30).

For Simon, the world becomes a stage, and the players are the animals and plants that find the promise of new life with the coming of spring. She is becoming a part of community life and nature as well. Modern conveniences become impractical and lose their allure.

After her first winter, Simon experiences community life in a different fashion: Vannie arrives to help her with work on the homestead. The mutually beneficial relationship materializes through Granny's initiative; Savannah will receive an education, which will include learning to be a proper young lady, and Simon will in turn learn all the skills needed for subsistence living. And along the way, Savannah gains Simon's friendship. She also receives necessities for social survival: shoes bought to convey social footing with peers in school, and clothes that will allow her to pass out of poverty in society. School in the valley lasts five months of the year, open to the community children three months in winter and two months in summer when the crops are in.

Simon accepts the mother role within the hill community willingly. One might question, does she do this to be accepted by the community, fulfilling her role as social mother? Perhaps Vannie and Bob Jenkins come to live with Simon simply for survival, just as she came to the land to persevere in times of adversity. By opening her heart and home, she endures the inevitable refrain of parenting: loving, and eventually letting go.

Community Justice for Crimes

In chapter VIII, Simon discusses shunning that occurs within the hill community because of family incest. She deals with not only the hard life of privation but also the evil that can invade a community when its isolation occurs outside the arm of justice. The author presents the question theoretically: When a community chooses to ignore a crime, shunning instead of confronting, who is accountable for its insidious growth and the moral decay it brings? Is it just the father, or also those who know his crime but remain silent? The image of an innocent child—depicted as a cherub with chubby features and "as fair as an angel"—lingers with Simon as the family who prompts her to consider how the "sins of our neighbors became our sins" passes by her cabin in their wagon, the reprehensible patriarch at the reins. Written in 1945, this is Simon's indictment: who will protect the innocent children from incestuous sexual crimes?

This episode opened the door to a topic that was generally closed tightly against public discussion; it stands as an example of Simon using her voice instead of continuing the silence. She reveals the hard and even evil side of poverty, and the scene, recounted ten years later, obviously haunts Simon. She clearly feels a deep sense of guilt for not intervening on behalf of the Long children, for her and the community's complicity in remaining silent. The image of nature giving judgment, expressed in hues of "red, like a bed of hot ashes" as the wagon leaves, embodies the rage and shame the community will confront only through shunning. Offering food and shelter is more than hospitality in the hill culture—it is an accepted code of conduct that is not violated. By refusing safe harbor to the family, even to the innocent children, Simon stands in solidarity with the justice meted by the hill community: silent condemnation.

The author offers another example of community justice for crimes in an opposite manner with Simon as the judge: the boy who served as the model for Simon's protagonist in *Robin on the Mountain* appears at her cabin and then becomes, in essence, her foster son. Bob Jenkins is an orphan who has run away from the orphanage in Little Rock, returning to see if his family might now be capable of taking care of him. After learning that his father has died and that none of his other kin still live in the community, the young boy persuades Simon to let him work as her handyman in exchange for a home. She accepts the responsibility of mothering this child, who became known for his acts of thievery when he was last a member of the hill community. In return, it is through this child that Simon confronts her own religious faith, brought back to prayer by a small boy who still feels the communication is important, regardless of the adversity he has seen in life:

"Don't we say our prayers before breakfast?" he asked.

I grew up at a time when it was smart to have no faith. We debunked everything and everybody. When we were through with all the heroes of history, we went on to God and the Saints. But even in my doubts, the most beautiful memory I had was of kneeling at my mother's knee, in a white cotton nightgown and my hair rolled up in rag curlers.... I lost something fine when I lost my belief in miracles, when I no longer thought that water could be turned to wine or Lazarus brought back from the dead.

It had been a long time since I had prayed. I turned to Vannie, but her eyes were like those of a child upon me. With two, now, looking to me for an example, I suddenly found it possible to turn again to the things I thought I had lost.

"Yes," I said to Bob. "We'll say our prayers before breakfast" (95–96).

This chapter of revival and second chances with Bob's "adoption" ends not only with the rain restoring life but also a foreshadowing of lightning striking near the cabin in the storm. Simon also includes a story of a small rabbit caught by the household cat. She is torn by Vannie's desire to keep the rabbit as a pet; Bob's desire to eat it, in light of their dwindling pantry; and the cat's desire to play with it, then eat it when it becomes too tired to fight any longer. Opening the door, Simon gives the rabbit a fighting chance to determine its own fate. This story foreshadows what occurs in the second half of the memoir with the children who arrived at her doorstep—and with Simon herself. Each individual comes to a crossroads; each character must determine his own path. And at each crossroads,

Simon is required to let go, even when she wants to hold on tightly and keep the memory, place, or the child as a "pet." Through this anecdote about the rabbit, the reader can recognize Simon's own struggle in choosing her path. Motivating Simon's initial return to the land was the search for a home, but also a search for herself. She discovers herself in her homesteading years, learning who she is at her core being. Poverty focuses her, allowing her to view the simple essentials of life, framing her philosophy on humankind. She is refined by life's adversities; as a survivor, she stands when others might have buckled under the pressure or caved to the demands of others.

Community Sustaining Its Members

In many of her novels for children, Simon shows the importance of community for survival during adversity. In *Straw in the Sun*, she illustrates the concept of community as a sustaining element through the activity of the harvest. Harvesting epitomizes the survival strategies of the hill people, who gather and store what can be found to survive on during the upcoming slim winter. Although the rain has ended the drought, the winter is bleak, as food stores are low. Simon and the children must turn to the forest and their neighbors for food that their winter pantry cannot provide.

Another example of the community sustaining its members comes when Granny Massery, Vannie's grandmother, joins their homestead family for an extended stay. Granny's presence provides a social commentary, speaking to the differences between her and her son in life, work, family, and charity; she is too proud to ask for help from others, even if circumstances are dire. Her son stands in contrast, willing to accept charity without shame, and lazy about exerting effort to improve the well-being of his family. In this example, Simon raises the question of nature versus nurture. What makes Jeff Massery a shiftless member of the community when his mother is a proud woman and a hard worker? Judged by the community in her youth as a woman whose child arrived "too soon after the wedding," Granny Massery refuses regret: "I've lived a long time . . . and there's little of life that I've missed. Still and all, I can't say there's a thing I've ever done I'm sorry for" (148).

Simon accepts Granny's philosophy as her own; significantly, Simon ultimately leaves her homesteading experience with this mentality. Granny has supplied the mentoring role model of one who is willing to stand firm in her convictions, unashamed and unapologetic, when the path she chose seemed to veer from what was expected according to society's norms. Granny's folk wisdom causes Simon to reflect on her own life: "I saw my reflection in the mirror staring back at me. And I wondered if all my life was behind me at thirty-three. Or was there a future ahead to look forward to. What was it and where would I find it? I wondered" (152). Here, viewing the nonbiological children who constitute her family in this Christmas scene, perhaps Simon is contemplating the role she will choose as a woman: will she embrace the wife and mother role, or will she pursue her dreams of a writing career? Possibly she is considering her biological clock and the maternal desire these foster children create.[2]

The community also sustains its members through gatherings and other rituals, as noted in the chapter where Simon attends a revival. When the women pray together, they create holy ground. It is a sacred feminine act that binds them closely together. The dance held at Simon's house feels much the same, a sacred communal moment. In their dancing, neighbors connect with each other spiritually, creating intimacy in community. Simon writes:

> My house was never so lovely to me as it was that night. A soft light shone from the oil lamps and the two blazing fires on the ceilings with their hand-hewn crossbeams and rafters, bringing out the rich, warm color of the pine. It brightened the women's dresses and the men's overalls as they surged in and out of the rooms. There was a smell of the earth in the room that night, and of men and women who live close to it. I felt a part of them, then. (159)

What Simon is experiencing is community, a closeness in space as well as spirit: she is accepted by the hill people in her homestead cabin, and the blessing of acceptance makes her house warm and lovely. Even the earthy smell of her neighbors becomes a welcome, intimate part of her; she is a part of them, and they are one.

Following the occasion of the folk dance, the need for community is fully revealed in the winter of suffering. This is the winter that tests Simon's character and perseverance in winning the bet with the government. She gives the perspective of a parent watching children suffer and her attempts to ease that suffering. During the winter of privation, Simon struggles with the tension between remaining a law-abiding citizen and fighting for survival: "It was not the hunting season, but I was in no mood to be told when I could or could not be hungry and feed hungry mouths dependent on me. Those laws were made by men in the cities, who came out to hunt, not because they needed meat, but because it gave them pleasure to kill" (176). Simon's

INTRODUCTION XXV

statement against the waste of the modern hunter stands in contrast to her hunting for necessity.

Although the winter is difficult to survive, it is the privation and survival skills gained while homesteading that fuel Simon's ability to become a published author.[3] Simon relates the generosity of the hill people and their commitment to helping each other through hard times, a characteristic she did not regularly witness in her daily life in New York City:

> These were the poor whites, the Wheelers, the Nixons, the Wells and the Widow Johnson, people who live in unpainted shacks and go barefoot in the summer, who wear patched clothes and smell of sweat and tobacco and cotton cloth. In some states they are called "Peckerwoods" or "Crackers." Cartoons are drawn about them and plays are written about them to make people laugh. But I lived through the rest of that winter, knowing a kindness and a generosity I had never known before, when, in their poverty, they shared the little they had with me and among themselves. (181)

Simon continues the theme of refusing to judge merely by appearance; community means getting to know the individuals instead of accepting surface stereotypes or caricatures. Sustaining each other through difficult times, the poor people in the hill community defy the stereotypes and labels given by society.

Following the privation, Simon shows the return of life after the long winter, declaring the miracle of the incipient spring. Spring flourishes for Simon in the regeneration of her garden, and the experience of survival through desperate times has changed Simon's perspective on life. She has learned what it means to be on the bottom rail, growing from

the experience in a manner that can be witnessed in the lives
of her fictional characters for the remainder of her life:

> Bob and Vannie read aloud as I lay on the grass to listen, and
> to tell them the meaning of words they stumbled over. From
> where I lay, I could see things I had not seen from higher up,
> a black cricket hopping through the flowers, an ant carrying
> a heavy burden as it walked over a grass blade, a pale green
> katydid like a leaf moving. I had seen things from the bottom
> that winter, in another way, things I would never have seen
> from higher up. I could look back now and call it a magnif-
> icent experience, one I would not have wanted to miss, but
> which I hoped never to have again. (183–84)

A unique experience has refined Simon during the hard
winter: she has seen things from the bottom and under-
stands the suffering she would have ignored in previous
years, when finances allowed her to lead a life of leisure.
While she finds hope and the promise of financial stability when a check for her published article arrives in the
mail, Simon still remembers the privation the winter created. An excursion to town with the children to buy supplies and clothing with the cashed check leaves her torn
between the draw of modernity in the city and the con-
nection of community with her hill neighbors—a community that rallied to support her and the children when
she had nothing to offer financially in return. Her choice
was clear as she returned to Rocky Crossing: "as I turned
the bend, I saw my log house behind the stake-an'-rider
fence. The two wings [that extended past the main room]
were like two arms held out to greet me. No bus to Little

Rock could tempt me now" (199). She was home and was not looking back at the life of leisure the city could provide. Without this experience in privation, Simon would have lacked the empathy that her novels of the Depression exhibit for those suffering in poverty. She now knew what it meant to go without food and to worry about mere survival. This would become a characteristic theme in all her fiction for children.

Although community sustains its members in the memoir, *Straw in the Sun* ends with Simon reflecting on the whereabouts of her former foster children. Bob had gone to live with his sister in a county nearby, to avoid having to return to the orphanage in Little Rock. Simon never hears from him again after this, as "the wilderness had drawn its curtain over him." This repetition of the excluding act of the wilderness reinforces the idea that Simon herself becomes lost to the hill people when she leaves her homestead.

In her writing style, there is a contrast in her speech when she retells the story of losing Bob. Perhaps the memory is too painful, even a decade later. The fact that she asks about him when the story returns to the present time at the memoir's end is indicative of the ever-present memory and loss. Told with stark and simple lines, Bob's leaving is even more impactful; the only passage that carries Simon's normal poetic prose recalls her watching his image disappear over the hill: "We saw Bob reach the top of the hill, then he went down, out of sight, first his legs, then his shoulders and his head. I thought of our mornings at the creek when he jumped in the water, disappearing from view, with ripples rising up from where he was. There was not even a ripple now, nor a splash to show where he went" (209). The mother's heart, even if only holding him for a season, was forever touched by this child who inspired her first book. In her time of grieving over the loss of the young boy, Simon begins to write her first fiction novel for children: "I wrote my first book at that time, and called it *Robin on the Mountain*. It was a book for children, the kind of story Bob liked to hear at night before he went to sleep. . . . The wilderness had drawn its curtain over him as it had done to his sister and to Mrs. Lewis when she left her old homeplace" (210–11).

To bring complete closure to the homesteading experience, the curtains are slowly closing. Bob is gone, and Simon begins her writing in attempt to compensate for this loss. Next Vannie leaves, traveling with her family to Coal Hill, where workers are needed for the mines.

When Simon returns to the homestead four years later with her husband John Gould Fletcher, it is clear that time has marched on, leaving the simpler times a nostalgic memory. The couple are bringing modern conveniences to the cabin, which they plan to live in full-time while their new home is being constructed on a wooded property overlooking the Arkansas River, eight miles outside of downtown Little Rock. Yet on the night before their scheduled move in, the cabin is struck by lightning and destroyed, burning completely to the ground. Significantly, when told the devastating news, Simon immediately thinks of arson: someone burned the cabin down to keep the wilderness closed to outsiders. Her first words upon receiving the news are "Gordon Hale." Hale was suspected to have burned down houses in the valley of those who were outsiders. Yet, she is assured Hale is dead.

Even if Hale is not responsible, she is coming back to
her homestead with indoor plumbing, a range, and other
"citified" amenities that signify bringing modernity to the
hills. All these threatening elements encroach upon the
survival of the independent hill community. She is an outsider who will live there only temporarily while her permanent home is being built in the city. Anyone who wishes
to protect their tight-knit community could commit arson
during a storm, with the alibi of a lightning strike as the
perfect cover-up. In this act of returning, Simon discovers
she is now an outsider.

Uncharacteristic of her writing style, the memoir ends
with two three-page chapters, compared to her normal
twenty-page chapters. It is as if closing the door to the
dreams of her homestead is still too painful, so she slams
it shut quickly instead of allowing a prolonged and painful goodbye. Simon learns that the young men she knew
while living at Rocky Crossing have all gone off to war. Bob
Jenkins had returned often to the valley and the cabin, coming back to Rocky Crossing alone before he left as a soldier.
Now he is fighting in the Solomon Islands in World War II.

Simon ends the book with a promise: she'll rebuild
Rocky Crossing for all the brave young men fighting in
the war, defending the valley's right to be closed off from
the world. And ironically, just as Bob foresaw, she does not
keep her promise of providing a home for him. Life moves
on and the wilderness closes in on the homestead, making
the ruined foundations that remain impossible to see from
the road that still passes through the land.

* * *

Publicity photo for *Straw in the Sun*. Series II, Box 5, File 5, Photo 259, *Charlie May Simon Papers, 1390-1977, UALR.MS.0006.*

So, how does *Straw in the Sun* remain relevant to readers in our twenty-first-century world? Or for that matter, what relevance does Charlie May Simon bring to our current reading public? Simon's memoir offers a unique perspective to those readers who remember a childhood accentuated by library trips in the summer, the pleasures of embarking on faraway adventures even when their feet remained planted at home. For the adults who affectionately remember Teeny Gay and her life on the riverboat, or Robin, who longed to help his sharecropper father, the exposure to Charlie May Simon as the real woman behind the fictionalized tales is invaluable. Her life, and her work, remain as an inspiration to persevere through life's hard times. Simon championed goodness over evil, peace over discord and war, and love for life, nature, and humankind: her message deserves reflection now more than ever. Good news and positivity are commodities in short supply; civil discourse and peaceful mediation for conflicting viewpoints are now rarely modeled.

In her diary, in March of 1974, Charlie May noted that "everything is beautiful, sparkling in color in spite of the rain." The following day, she balanced the negative report of "cold outside" with the positive contrast of "but I can never tire [of] looking out the window at the beauty of spring." During a health crisis in May of the same year, she recorded, "I hope, whatever they find, there is a cure for it. Life is sweet."⁴ The voice of Charlie May Simon remains relevant, serving as a reminder that during life's struggles, there is always beauty to be discovered. True to the mantra held by her fictional characters, and by those depicted in her biographies and memoirs, the author Charlie May Simon believed that "life is sweet" if one perseveres through adversity.

Notes

1. Howard was physically present in the homestead experience yet is a "ghost" in Simon's memoir, mentioned only by the young boy at the picnic who refers to "they," not "she." Howard also wrote a memoir of homesteading, three decades after *Straw in the Sun* was published, and neither Charlie May nor the children are present in the solitary experience he recounts.

2. It is clear from correspondence before their marriage that John Gould Fletcher wanted children with Charlie May, yet his obituary noted the fact that their marriage did not provide children ("Noted Arkansas Poet Discovered Dead in Water," *Daily Oklahoman*, May 11, 1950, 15). It is significant to recognize that Charlie May was in her late thirties and early forties when she wrote the memoir, not the young woman of thirty-three in the mirror she remembers in this scene. The author is possibly reflecting that her opportunity for motherhood has ended. However, it is unclear in her correspondence whether her desire to be a mother reflected her mother's dream or her own, unattained.

3. Simon speaks of writing "Retreat to the Land: An Experience in Poverty" (reproduced in Appendix A; *Scribner's Magazine* 93, no. 5 [May 1933]) "before she knew the people well," which could account for the change in her perspective from "outsider" in the article to "insider" in *Straw in the Sun*.

4. Charlie May Simon, "Appointment diary, 1974: March 24–26, May 29," Series II, Box 2, Folder 6, Charlie May Simon Papers, 1390-1977, UALR.MS.0006.

STRAW IN THE SUN

Chapter I

LAST spring I went to Rocky Crossing again. New green grass was sprouting on the high ridge of the road that led there, and now and then there grew a persimmon shoot, or a small hickory, where a nut had fallen and opened deep in the untrampled earth. But the ruts made long ago by passing wagons were still there, guiding the wheels of our car through the dense forest, around the boulders and between the tall trees.

I was like a ghost returning to a place once loved. I wondered if ghosts, too, brought friends of their new existence with them as I had wanted to do, and if they said with pride, as I am now saying, "Behind the house there was a rose garden, with a lily pond where wild iris grew."

The roses were in bloom. They were the old-fashioned kind that came out in a riot of pink and red and white only once a year. But it was worth waiting fifty weeks for the next blooming. The stonewall that once surrounded the rose garden, built to shut out the wilderness, had crumbled and the rocks lay scattered over the ground. Like an army of marching soldiers, the wilderness had come to the very border, and there it stopped. The growing trees stood close together, and were so thick, even with their small new leaves of spring, that the path leading to the huckleberry patch was lost.

One tree had broken rank, a red oak shoot that grew beside the moss rose. Through force of habit, I reached down to pull it out.

The wilderness and I had made a bargain, which we both had kept. But we worked hard, each to make the other live up to his side. The homeplace, with its barnyard and vegetable patch and rose garden, was to be mine. All the rest of the sixty acres belonged to the forest. The roots of the trees had been like dragons' teeth, sending up ten for each one cut down. I had pulled and chopped, until finally they gave up and died, but only on my side of the fence. On the other side, the trees dropped new seeds every year, and pine and hickory and oak saplings came up to take the place of the old and dying ones.

On the place where the house once stood, two stone chimneys faced each other with their black mouths opened wide. Wild flowers grew between them. There were violets, but they were like old ladies in faded dresses, now that their season was over, and the sweet Williams had come to take up their pattern of color. The fallen stones of the foundation marked the outline of the rooms, ending with the stone-paved patio where the well still stood with the climbing red rose tangled around it.

We spread a picnic lunch on the ground and sat on Mexican serapes to eat it. A young rabbit crouched near one of the chimneys, still and frozen, pretending it was part of the earth and stones. Only its quivering nose and protruding eyes turning backward and forward and on all sides, showed it was a thing alive. When it saw we were coming no closer, it scurried off through the grass and disappeared from sight. A jay flew over our heads, and another flew after, screaming angrily. Then he turned around and gave chase himself. These two were fighting over their rights to my property.

We were on a high ridge. The land sloped down and then up again, to the north and south of us, and we could see far out over the distant mountains to the faint blue peaks beyond. Cove creek ran to the west of us, but it was hidden by the dense forest. The sound of the water was lost in the sound of wind blowing through the trees, and we had to listen closely to know which was the water and which was the wind. Even when the creek was high, the water was blue and clear, and we could see the jagged rocks on the bottom, that gave my home its name.

Once I had been part of this landscape. Its life and mine were one. The rabbits crouching still and frozen and the jays fighting for their property rights, were also one with me.

A clump of spiderwort grew among the old foundation stones, and one, the first of the season, had opened like a bright blue eye staring at a new-made world. John got up to pick it and he brought it to me.

"Vannie didn't like the name 'spiderwort,' " I said. "She called them blue-eyed Marys."

"That is a much better name," John agreed.

I talked of Vannie then, and of Bob, and of those who had helped make the place a home. And I described Rocky Crossing as it had been. But you can tell a story a hundred times, and each one who hears it sees a different picture in his mind until it becomes a hundred different stories. Even those who know me best, cannot see Rocky

Crossing as I saw it, nor the people who made it the place that it was. It is like coming upon a pressed bouquet of flowers, tied with a tattered and faded ribbon, and holding each dry flower up to tell of how it looked when it was fresh and alive.

When we had finished our lunch of fried chicken and stuffed eggs, and had drunk hot coffee from thermos jars, we walked to the old vegetable garden. The wilderness had kept its bargain there, too. But the rains and frost had brought rocks up from the ground, and again, through force of habit, I picked them up and piled them on the sloping side.

A heap of rotting logs was all that was left of the chicken house, but I wanted to see it again to end a dream that had been haunting me for the eight years since I had left Rocky Crossing. Sometimes it occurs several nights in succession, and again months will pass before it comes back. In my dreams I return to Rocky Crossing and find some animal I have neglected, dead or dying of hunger and thirst. Sometimes it is Zozo, the dog, or the pig or calf. But more often it is the flock of chickens that I find lying weak and bony, panting their last. Their eyes look at me reproachfully as I hasten to bring water and food to them. But I am always awake before I know whether it has done any good. At first I awoke with the feeling of guilt still with me. But since the dream has come so many times, I now awaken angry. After all, the forest is full of food for chickens and dogs and calves, and there is water at Cove creek which these animals could reach if they would bestir themselves, instead of waiting for me to come back to them in my dreams.

A wood thrush sang in the distance. The song of the cardinal, the mocking bird, or the Carolina wren is one of love and desire and the joy of living. But the song of the wood thrush is a sweet anthem of praise. That night the angels sang "Peace on earth, good will to men," it must have sounded to the shepherds who listened like the music of the wood thrush.

Suddenly a shot was fired and the bird stopped short in its song. The whole forest was hushed. Not a song was heard nor a footstep on the twigs and leaves. We knew, though we could not see, that every wild creature of the woods was waiting in silence, as still as the rabbit that had been in our path, smelling that dreaded smell of man and gun and dog. Then, as if at a given signal, a squirrel jumped from one bough of a tree to another and the jay flew toward its nest with a worm. The wood thrush took up its song once more, and a dove cooed in accompaniment.

A dog came running toward us, appearing suddenly as if he had sprung up from the ground. But he would have none of our advances. He sniffed at our feet, and there was not the familiar smell of blue denim and tobacco about us that he had found here, even on strangers, and he backed away when I put out my hand to stroke him. To the dog, too, I was a trespasser on my own property. He ran back to his young master, now turning the bend in the road.

The boy nodded shyly when he saw us. He was barefoot, and wore blue denim overalls, and he carried a shotgun. He might have been any one of the boys I used to know who came to these woods to hunt and fish and trap when I lived here. I searched his face for some familiar feature, but eight years ago he could not have been more than a child, with round baby features not yet formed by his character.

"How is the hunting?" we asked.

"Not bad," he replied.

He sat on a rock beside us and we talked of hunting and of fishing at the creek. He was shy, and answered in monosyllables at first. But, like most shy people, he wanted to be in the company of others so he lingered on.

"That was a good house before it burned," the boy said, looking toward the two stone chimneys. "Struck by lightning two years ago, and burned plumb to the ground just the night before the lady that used to live here was coming back."

He told it as if it had been a story told many times, and I knew that when the valley people got together and talked of strange things that happened, they talked about my house at Rocky Crossing.

Before the fire had come suddenly out of the storm to strike my house, it had stood vacant for six years. It was the only house for six miles on either side, and it had provided shelter for all who passed that way. Hunters had camped there, and lumberjacks, cutting timber on adjoining land, had made it their home. Cows and mules and even deer that roamed the mountainside came in when the doors were left open, to get out of the rain.

The boy had passed here many times and, in his imagination, he must have pictured the place as it was when it was the home of living people, just as I had once drawn mental pictures of the old Lewis homeplace. I kept quiet while he talked, for I remembered my disappointment when Mrs.

Lewis returned, and I had found her not at all as I thought she would be.

"Once I came when they lived here," the boy said. "But I was so little then, all I remember was a cake with some leaves and matches on it."

Chapter II

ROCKY CROSSING was created out of a need for a home. There was still land free for homesteading in 1931. All one needed do was to select his site from the land available, put in his claim at the nearest land office, build a habitable house and cultivate and fence a reasonable portion of the land. After living there seven months a year for three years, he could go back to the land office and have title to his acres.

A map in a land office, with numbers and letters on it, is cold and impersonal. It was not until I was on the place, with my feet on the ground, that 5½ N E N E N W 24-3-20 changed from a slip of white paper to a place of green forests and a clear running creek, with a rocky bed, and hills in the distance where white clouds passed like giant sheep grazing in a blue pasture. My home was here before me. The tall straight pines would make its walls and roof, the stones would make the chimneys to keep me warm, and the earth, with its thick mulch of leaves and pine needles, would produce the food I needed.

Sixty-six years before, my grandfather had passed down this road with his wife and two little girls, looking for a place to build his home, as I was doing. There were things that he, too, wanted to forget. The long war was over and behind him, and there was a new life to begin. And for my grandmother, who had plowed and harvested and had done all the work of a man as well as the spinning and weaving and caring for the two babies, there would be no more nights of waiting and wondering if he would ever come back. There was only the future to think about.

They passed through my sixty acres, then unsurveyed, and went down in the valley to stake their claim. Here other children were born and grew up and married, to raise families of their own. The girls stayed on, but the boys went out in the world, worked their way through to a higher education, and settled in the cities.

The people of the valley still remembered my grandparents. They accepted me as Old Doc Hogue's granddaughter who had come back home. And they helped me build my house and fence and plow the garden patch.

I had dreamed the plans of my house for a long time, but there were no blueprints for the men to go by. Instead, I drew it all out with a stick in the dirt, measuring each room with a long, steel tape measure.

"Here is the living room," I said, drawing a rectangle twenty-six feet by seventeen. "And here is the dining room." I extended the line sixteen feet longer across the front, setting it back to form a wing. There was a stone chimney at one end of the dining room and one at the other end of the living room, so that they stood facing each other through the wide open doorway. The kitchen was behind the dining room, and across the patio there was a bedroom and wash room, forming a wing on the other side of the living room.

No one here had seen a house quite like it before, but they put up the logs of peeled pine, with notches cut so true we could scarcely see where they were joined together. And they cut out the doors and windows where I told them to cut.

Uncle George Nixon, who kept the general store and post office, down in the valley, first showed me where the land lay. He spread the news of my coming and sent the men to build the house. But the first who came was one he had not sent. He was Gordon Hale, a lean, sour-faced man who had come as a stranger to the valley many years before. He came to dig the well but after the first day he left, saying it would have to be drilled, and he never came back.

"Gordon Hale just wanted to look you over to make sure you wouldn't be bothering about his still down in the narrows," Uncle George told me afterward.

It was several days before I could piece together the names and faces and personalities of these people who were to be my only friends and neighbors from now on. It was like starting a jigsaw puzzle, taking each piece up and examining it to see where it fit, wondering in the end why you had not known it all along. They were dressed alike, in blue overalls, some new and some faded and patched, and blue jumpers which they removed in the heat of the day.

There was old Jock Wheeler, sitting on a tree stump, making shingles from a large pine sawed in two-foot lengths. He wore a long mustache, and his blue eyes, the color of the outdoors, were set deep in a nest of wrinkles. He worked alone without saying a word until the noon hour, when he quit to eat his lunch from a tin lard bucket. Then the other men brought their lunches and squatted beside him, listening while he talked, and now and then joining in with yarns of their own. Like all men who do not, or cannot read, they were good listeners and tellers of tales.

"That time old Daddy Means was stalking a bear," his slow drawl was a signal for all talking to stop. "Wasn't nothing but a big old coon's tracks he saw in the snow, but he swore it was a bear. Said he ought to know, he'd hunted enough bear in his time. Well, he walked all day from sun-up till sundown. I came on his tracks along about here where I'm sitting, and I could tell he was worn to a frazzle by the way those footsteps dragged. I slipped up behind him, quiet and easy so he wouldn't hear me, and I put my arms around his waist in a tight bear hug. And derned if he didn't faint dead away, and I had to tote him all the way home."

There was loud laughter and another story followed about Daddy Means. He was my nearest neighbor on the other side of the creek, I was told, and a queer-turned fellow he was. He had come here long ago in his youth, and staked out his claim. No one knew who he was nor where he was from. That was his own secret which he kept to himself, but it was said that he could not read or write, and he made his mark with a cross.

The men had no watches, but a glance at the sun told them how long they had spent over their lunches of biscuits and molasses and fried salt meat.

Jeff Massery, tall and bony with skin the yellow color of malaria, was the last to get up. Lazily he stretched himself and got into his wagon to take up the reins, and lazily the old mule pulled him down to the creek to bring back a load of sand to be mixed with the cement. It would be hours before I saw him again, I knew. Though the creek was close by, two loads a day were all I could expect.

The other men took pride in their work. They cut the straightest pines of the forest and peeled them, and when Jeff's mule was too slow in dragging them to the home site, they lifted them by hand, each trying to show his strength. Rufus Wells was the strongest. His son Bill worked with him, but he left soon to go to the county seat, where he attended school.

"Took a notion to go to high school there, and nothing could stop him," Rufus said. "Works all winter there to pay his keep."

Once every man laid down his tools and went off in search of a bee tree. It was during the noon hour, when old Jock Wheeler was telling a yarn to the men squatting beside him. A bee lit on Jeff Massery's hand to sip the sorghum that dripped from his biscuit. He held his hand as still as the hand of a statue, and all eyes were fastened on the bee. Old Jock Wheeler stopped short in his tale as the bee, having sipped its fill, rose high in the air and circled around to get its bearings. When it flew off toward the narrows, in a straight line, they got up, to a man, and followed it with axes and their empty lunch buckets. When they returned, an hour or so after sundown, they offered no apology for having abandoned me. They had worked because they wanted to work and they quit when they wanted to quit. The golden honey in the pail which they gave me was not given as compensation. It was given in the spirit of one neighbor sharing his good fortune with another.

When the fishing was good, they went off to fish, and when the blackberries were ripest, there was no work done on the house for several days. The men went off with their families, camping on old fields where the blackberries grew, and helped the children gather them while their wives cooked them in an iron pot over an open fire, and put them up in jars. The money I paid the men was more than enough to buy all the honey and fish and berries they needed, but this was their pleasure and they took it.

My first night at Rocky Crossing was spent in the dining room, with a doorway cut in the logs to let me in. I slept on the dirt floor, with the stars shining down between the rafters and a gentle wind blowing through the cracks between the logs. I might as well have slept outdoors, but it was pleasant to have my own walls about me. By the next night, more logs were added to form more rooms, and the shingles old Jock Wheeler had split made a roof over my head.

Gradually the house took shape, with windows and doors and a floor. And the furniture—the tables and chairs and bedsteads—was made of rough lumber, planed by hand, which I stained the color of old pine.

I came to rely upon Rufus Wells, the blacksmith of the valley. His thick, blunt hands were never still. He planed rough lumber to make the batten doors and he made strap hinges of iron for them. And during his lunch hour, when he had finished eating, he took out his sharp knife and whittled long wooden hinges for the Dutch door in the kitchen.

I could understand, now that I knew him, why the old French peasants had the saying, "Work is a prayer." To Rufus Wells work, like prayer, was not a thing to be used for bartering. It was his right.

My house was never quite complete. There were always things to dream of adding some day: a screen porch, more closets and perhaps even plumbing at some far-off time. But it was home to me, the home I had always wanted, and it was made of the things of the earth, of trees and stones and the labor of my neighbors. All I needed to buy from town were nails, windowpanes and screens, cement, and oil and turpentine and powdered colors to mix the stain. The lumber for the floors and sills and ceilings was sawed at a lumber mill, not many miles away. Now I was standing on my own land, with a home of my own, and the only price I had to pay was work with my hands and less than five hundred dollars in money.

Chapter III

ANIMALS have a way of communicating with one another without the use of sound. There must have been many silent messages speeding through the forest, of strange things happening on the ridge above the salt lick in the narrows, when I first came to Rocky Crossing. Before the house was even finished, there came the flies and wasps and yellow jackets. They liked the shelter it gave them. Their only objection was my presence there, and they did all they could to drive me away. When I sat down to my meals they hovered possessively over the sugar bowl and the honey dish, and resented having to share the sweets with me. But when the screens were put in place, they gave up and left me alone.

A herd of mules, ringing their bells as they grazed on the hillside, were my next visitors. When they saw a house where a house had never stood before, they stopped in their tracks and stared with a look of almost human curiosity in their eyes. It was such a stare as little children have when their parents have to whisper to them not to be rude. They came as close as they dared, to make sure their eyes had not deceived them. A little sorrel mare was with them, and I put out my hand to stroke her, but she went bounding away, and the others followed, with bells jingling in every key.

The cows that came were not so shy. They looked in my windows and through the open door, and when I drove them away, they only pretended to leave. As soon as my back was turned, there they were, at my window again, watching my every move. They came every day until the stake and rider fence was built to keep them out. By then they had grown used to the house and the city-bred, wire-haired terrier that romped outside. They passed by, with only side glances as they bent their heads to graze.

There were other animals, too, staring with the same curiosity, and I could feel their eyes looking down from the trees or from behind boulders, though I could not see them. This ridge was far enough from the valley settlement so that the deer and turkey, and the wolves, wild cats and foxes felt safe to roam here. These creatures were my only neighbors for six miles on either side. Zozo, the dog, knew them better than I, by the smell of their tracks on the soft earth.

It was through the death and funeral of a newborn baby that I came to know my human neighbors down in the valley, the families of the men who built the house at Rocky Crossing. On the first cold day of autumn, I went down for my mail, but there was no one in the post office. The porch was empty, too, with the squirrel tails that hung from the rafters blowing softly in the wind, and the chairs leaning against the wall. A mouse was gnawing wood somewhere in the room, and it stopped suddenly when I entered. Then I heard the faint talk of women from a room beyond the store, and there was a sound of hammering in the barn across the road with the drone of men's voices accompanying it. I went to the barn in search of Uncle George Nixon, and I found him there with the other men of the valley I had come to know. They were sawing and nailing together a little narrow box of rough pine lumber.

"I could have told you that piece was too short," Uncle George was saying to Rufus Wells who threw down a piece of wood in disgust.

"Like old Daddy Means," Jock Wheeler said. "He was making a coffin for Ben Leach and blamed if he didn't try to narrow it down to fit the old man's wooden leg."

A man with a red beard and keen blue eyes, and fine features that looked like George Bernard Shaw, if one could imagine an untidy Shaw, smiled sheepishly and said, "Now that ain't so."

The men laughed, then their faces were sober again, as if they had done wrong to laugh. They looked up when I entered, and spoke to me, then they went on with their work.

"The womenfolks are in the back room, behind the store," Uncle George said.

I was beginning to learn that women did not go where men were gathered together. Their place was with the other women. I found them in the back room, sitting on two beds and on straight chairs brought in from the kitchen. The pine walls had mellowed a dark, rich color, and they were hung all over with bright calendars and advertisements that had been sent to the store. One of the women was sewing on a dress so small it might have been a doll's dress, and another was making a little cap of the same material. The others were tearing an old sheet into strips and scalloping the edges.

There were no introductions. The women accepted me as my grandmother was accepted. I was one of them and there was no need to say any more about it. Jock Wheeler's wife moved over and made room for me on the bed beside her and she gave me scissors and a strip of cloth to scallop.

"It's the Massery baby," old Mrs. Nixon said, turning to me. "Born last night after sundown, and it went like this." She gave the start of a cry and stopped short. "That's the way it went and then it died."

The other women began to talk, telling me of Mag Massery's labors, for they had all been present to help at the child's birth.

"The screech owls made a racket like I never heard before, and a whippoorwill landed right on the roof and called, late in the year as it is," Mrs. Wheeler put in.

"That old grey cat was in the room and it looked square at the little one right after it had washed its face," a quiet-voiced woman spoke up, and I learned she was Rufus Wells' wife. They talked in awed voices of signs of death, and their faces were more serious than the faces of the men, for they had seen the baby try to come into the world and fail.

Uncle George Nixon came in with the coffin, and the women padded the inside with cotton, which they covered with part of the torn sheet. Then they tacked the scalloped edges, one strip overlapping the other, around the sides. When it was finished, the men joined us and we walked the mile to the Massery house.

The house had one room, with a lean-to kitchen. The room was heated with a stove made from an old iron oil drum. A tin stovepipe led from a hole cut in the drum to a hole cut in the wall. There was no furniture except two iron beds, a trunk and a straight-back chair. A few dresses and overalls hung limply from nails driven in the wall. Mag

Massery, tired and old at thirty-five, lay in one of the beds, with a little girl about four sitting beside her playing with a stick whittled to look like a doll. On a packing box at the foot of the bed, with a sheet spread over it, the dead baby lay like a wax doll some child had grown tired of and put aside. A long slant of sunlight came through the open door to light the room, with countless particles of air dancing in it like creatures alive.

Jeff Massery got up from the chair when we came in, to make room for us. There was a dignity about him now, with death touching one of his own, and we spoke with awe and respect to him.

Mrs. Wheeler took the baby in her arms and put on him the little dress and cap to match. Then she laid him in the box.

"Ain't he pretty," a bright-eyed little old woman said, coming in from the kitchen. "Here, Mag, don't he look like a little angel."

She brought the coffin close to the bed for Mag Massery to see, and the little girl got up to look, too. A young girl, with delicate features very much like the old woman's, except that her dark eyes were more dreamy and shy, had followed her in from the kitchen.

"Here, Vannie, hold Ona up and let her touch the little one," the old woman said.

The girl took little Ona in her arms and leaned over the body of the dead child.

"Touch him here, honey," she whispered.

She put the child's hand on the baby's forehead, then she touched it again with her own hand. One by one the others came up and gently touched the corpse.

"Better touch him too, so you won't dream about the dead tonight," Mrs. Wheeler said to me.

The men took the coffin outside and we could hear the sounds of nails being driven in the lid to close it.

"I plumb forgot to put the pillow in," Mrs. Nixon said. It was too late. The lid was on and the little one must lie from now on with no pillow at his head.

We were a strange procession as we retraced our steps along the road, printing the frosty ground with our footsteps. The day was cold and the men wore two pairs of overalls, with the faded ones showing under the bright, new ones. Their blue mingled with the browns and reds and greens of our coats and dresses. Zozo trotted ahead, with her tail held high like a plume. She was a city dog, but she was not a stylish one, for a wire-haired terrier should have no tail, and hers was long.

We came to the cemetery, where a white building of one room, which served as church and school, stood on a hill above it. A grave had been dug under a dogwood tree, and the little coffin was placed inside. A flock of cedar waxwings, migrating south, were perched in the tree eating the red berries, and they flew away, startled at our approach. They hovered about, watching and waiting impatiently for us to leave. There were other graves all about us, known only by the rise and fall of the earth. There were no headstones, but here and there a grave was marked by rocks around it, and broken bits of pottery and colored glass, a relic of the days when wolves came prowling among the graves of the dead.

There was no hymn sung and no prayer spoken, as dirt was thrown on the little pine box. But the lips of those about me moved in soft whispers, and I joined them in a silent prayer to send the little one on its way.

I thought of the poor, bare room we had left, of the shiftless father and the worn mother, and I wondered if the child were not better off never to have lived at all. Then I thought of Abraham Lincoln, born in just such a poor, bare room, of just such a shiftless father and tired, worn mother.

All during the burial, when the dirt was thrown back into the grave, I could feel the dark, shy eyes of the girl Vannie searching mine. After she had gone on back home with her grandmother, I could still see them in my mind. They were more haunting to me than my thoughts of the dead child.

We turned away and those that were with me took care not to point toward any of the graves, for whoever did would be the next one buried.

We didn't want to part just then and go back to our homes. Something had drawn us together, and we wanted to keep it so. We lingered on at the post office. Jeff Massery was there, buying flour and lard and salt pork.

"I'll pay you for sure," he was saying, "just as soon as——"

"Forget it, Jeff," Uncle George replied. "You don't owe for this."

We stepped aside respectfully when Jeff Massery walked out, and he held his head high with a new dignity.

The mail did not mean much to me now. I opened it and read it and the news from the outside seemed strangely unimportant. The sun went down, throwing its gold and red to the broken clouds which caught and held it, reluctant to let it go. And we were reluctant to go, too. We stayed on until the last color had faded and the whole earth was one dove-grey.

"Better just stay all night," Mrs. Nixon said to us all.

The widow Johnson with her six small sons stayed, but the others went on, saying as they left, "There's the stock to feed. We'd best be getting on. But you come home with us."

When the men were working on my house, each one said, as he left, "Better come go home and spend the night with us."

I had come to look upon it as a kind of ritual, a way of saying "good-bye." But now I saw a loneliness in the eyes of these people, and I felt that loneliness too, to be with them. We came to the Wheeler house, and Jock Wheeler said, "Come on in and spend the night with us."

I went in with them, and Daddy Means joined us. He went out to the barn with Jock and his son Ben to feed the animals while Mrs. Wheeler and I cooked the supper. We had black-eyed peas and baked sweet potatoes, and hot corn-bread with rich, yellow butter and all the buttermilk we could drink.

The Wheeler house had two large square rooms with a wide dog run between. The kitchen was built behind it, after the days of detached kitchens, and it was large enough to serve as dining room, too. When we had finished with our supper and the dishes were washed and put away, we went back to the main house, taking our chairs with us. The room had been recently papered with fresh newspapers and wherever possible, a colored page from the mail-order catalogs or an almanac was added, with a pretty girl in a swing, wearing a stylish dress, or a baby reaching out for a box of

STRAW IN THE SUN   25

talcum. With the printed word on the walls all around us, it was like being in a library with all the books opened. But we could not turn the pages. If we started to read how Greta Garbo eluded the reporters in New York or how the bank robbers entered a bank, we could never know what happened in the end.

"Now mind you, I don't believe there's such a thing as a ghost," Jock Wheeler said when we drew our chairs close to the fire, "but I tell you, I saw old man Leach standing before me, just three days after he died, as plain as I see you now."

The fire burned low and the shadows of the beds and bureau and chairs joined our shadows in a weird dance on the wall. Bunches of home-grown tobacco, hanging from the mantel, swayed in the heat of the ashes. Outside there was the sound of a screech owl, like the screaming laughter of a mad woman. Ben and Daddy Means turned the pockets of their overalls inside out and wrung them to wring the neck of the owl, but it had no effect. It went on with its shriek. It was easy to believe anything then, even in the return of old man Leach from his grave. The noise of the owl was not associated with a harmless grey bird that slept quietly in a stolen nest all day. It could have been a disembodied sound coming through the darkness of the night.

The clock on the mantel was old, bought in the days when the Yankee peddler came even to the hills of Arkansas. It had not run for many years, but we knew it was late and time to go to bed, for we began to yawn, each catching a yawn from the other. The fire had burned low while we listened to the tales Jock Wheeler told of other deaths in the valley and the ghosts he had seen.

The men went out at last, and I thought they had gone to the room across the way to sleep. Mrs. Wheeler and I undressed and got in bed, Mrs. Wheeler in one and I in the other and the men returned soon after. I had turned my face to the wall, and I could see their shadows, tall and grotesque, moving in the flicker of the dying ashes as they took off their overalls. Old Jock got into bed with his wife, and Ben and Daddy Means slept on a pallet on the floor. I closed my eyes then, and there came to me the two dark eyes of Vannie Massery staring shyly at me.

I slept a dreamless sleep. The sun was rising over the hills when I woke up in an empty room. Young Bennie and Daddy Means had gone off in the woods with dogs, before day, and had brought back a possum for breakfast. And Mrs. Wheeler mixed a ginger cake which we had with baked possum and sweet potatoes. It was a delicious meal to break our night's fast.

A new day had come. The funeral of the newborn baby belonged to yesterday. Now I must go back to Rocky Crossing. Daddy Means set off through the woods on his jenny, and I took the dirt road that led up the hill.

"Better come home and spend the night with me," I said as I left, after the custom of the people.

"We've a right smart to do around the place," Mrs. Wheeler replied. "But you just stay on here with us."

When I said I could stay no longer, she whispered something to her husband and he brought me a burlap bag with a mother hen and eight little chicks in it.

"Folks moving in a new house ought to have something to give them good luck," she said.

Chapter IV

THE first winter at Rocky Crossing passed quietly. I was busy every day, for there were so many things to be done to make my home complete; furniture to be painted, soft cushions to make for the chairs and sofa, braided rag rugs and gay colored curtains. Each day was like the day before, and I was absorbing my surroundings without being aware of it. Sometimes I drove to Little Rock to buy the things I needed. I belonged to two worlds then. I had accepted the solitude of Rocky Crossing with its deep forest where the wild animals were hidden, and the clear running water of the creek. And I had not given up the paved sidewalks and the street lights and the crowds brushing past me in the city. That was soon taken away from me.

One morning when I went down to the valley for my mail, I found a very embarrassed George Nixon. He cleared his throat several times as if there were something he wanted to say, but could not. It was strange to see this big, bluff man, who could swear and shout without hesitation, become suddenly shy. He gave me my mail with his eyes avoiding mine as if it were something he was ashamed to give me. I opened a letter from a department store, telling me a check I had given them had been returned, and would I please remit the amount due right away.

"How can that be?" I said, half to myself. "There's that money in the bank."

"That bank's failed," Uncle George said, simply.

It was some time before I could grasp the meaning of his words. It had not seemed much in the city when I left to come here. It was the last of money left me by someone dear to me, and it was fast dwindling away. But here, even after my house was built, it was more than enough to last until I owned the land and could sell the timber on it.

"Don't let that worry you," Uncle George was saying. "I know how it is. I had to borrow the five dollars it took me to homestead my land when I first married. I started out with nothing, not even nails to put up the house."

Through the open doorway I could see his cattle in the pasture, grazing on the drying grass and wading in the pond for a drink. Uncle George was a rich man by mountain standards, rich in land and cattle, which was the only way he counted riches. But he had acquired this by hard work.

"Now if there's anything you want," again he hesitated as if he were ashamed to speak the words. "If I can let you have anything to tide you over——"

When I had gone to town last I had drawn out a hundred dollars to keep at home with me for the things I needed at the valley store. I made figures in my mind, subtracting from that the amount I owed the department store in Little Rock. Then something else occurred to me.

"That check I gave you last week," I said. "Has that come back, too?"

"Hell, I'll get my money out of them that's to blame," he

was his old blustering self again. "Damned if I'll take it from you twice when they're the ones that's got it."

It was only a small amount, and after persuading him to take it and sending a money order to the department store, I had seventy-five dollars and a few cents left. That must last a long time.

I bought the animals I needed to supply me with food, ten barred rock hens and a rooster from Uncle George, for five dollars, and a baby pig for a dollar. It was a female pig with the masculine name of Adolphus.

"You don't need to buy a cow, with all the cows in the valley eating their heads off," Uncle George said. "I'd call it a favor if you'd take yonder brindle heifer of mine and let her get some of that mountain grass."

I led the brindle cow by a rope the ten miles to my house, with her newborn calf, curly and shining, leaping about and coming back now and then to nudge at her mother's side, in search of more food. The cow stood in silent contempt that evening, knowing that I had never milked before. She lapped her black nose with her long tongue, and swished her tail, and held back the milk until I turned her in with the calf.

News spreads fast in an isolated settlement where there are no newspapers. The story was told of my loss when the bank failed, and the amount grew with each telling. Then it was that I learned it is the poor who are the more generous, and who offer their friendship more readily.

Rufus Wells built a chicken house and a shed of logs, with a picket fence around it, for the calf. And he made a fence for the garden patch. Jock Wheeler split the pickets from pine logs, for him. But neither would accept the money I offered them.

"Building a house is one thing," Rufus Wells said. "I'd take money for that. But helping a neighbor put up a little old chicken house, that's another thing."

Something went wrong with the clutch band of the automobile, and there was no mechanic for thirty-five miles. Then the battery died from lack of use. The automobile stood in the yard, a useless piece of machinery. It was just as well, for there was no money to buy gasoline to run it. My old life was behind me now, and I became aware of the new. I was closer to the foxes that had their den near the hollow sycamore and the deer that came to the narrows for the salty taste of the earth there.

I began to notice things that I had not seen before. Spring came earlier to me than it ever had, for in other years it came with green grass in the park, birds building their nests in city trees, and jonquils and violets in the florist shop windows. But that year I saw it come in January, when it was still cold enough to button my coat tight against the north wind. I saw the buds swell with new life on the bare limbs of trees, I heard the first call of the frog after the rain, and I saw the earth turned up, under the dry, winter grass, by earthworms and insects that had been buried in its warmth and darkness. It was like sitting in a darkened theater, waiting for the play to begin. The orchestra marches in, the fiddles begin to tune, and you sit waiting, with a thrill of expectancy. At last the lights go out, the curtain slowly rises, and the play is on.

It was at this time that I came to know still another neighbor, one who was nearer than those in the valley to me. I

knew all about her, though she did not know of my existence, for she was a ghost neighbor. I had gone for a walk
in the woods, looking for a dogwood and redbud to trans-
plant in my own yard. Zozo ran ahead, smelling each fresh
track along the way. I came upon the faint trace of an old
path, covered over with pine needles, but the earth was so
beaten down by footsteps of long ago that no grass or seedlings grew over it now. I followed it until I could see ahead
of me a clearing where the sun filtered through the branches
of the trees like daylight through the window of a dark
room. The past was there, waiting for me, and it came out
to meet me when I entered the clearing. On each side of the
path, rows of jonquils sent up their pointed leaves, with
here and there a greenish bud ready to open on the first
warm day. They led to two climbing roses, lying sprawled
on the ground with nothing to climb on now.

Someone had once lived here, I knew, and I could feel
the presence of living beings around me as one does in a
house once lived in and deserted. But I could find no trace
of a house anywhere. There were not even the remains of a
chimney. Lilacs and burning bushes grew in a rectangle,
as plants grow around a foundation, showing me where the
house once stood.

It must have been a log house, with the logs long since
decayed, and the chimneys of stick and mud had now crumbled and were lost in the earth. It was not a large house. I
knew its size by the way the burning bushes and lilacs grew.
There was a spring a few hundred feet from where the
house had stood, with a path leading to it. There was another path that led from the spring to some rose bushes kept

pruned by the herds of mules and cows that passed here on
their way to the salt lick in the narrows.

Coming unexpectedly upon this old abandoned homeplace was like meeting a new neighbor I had not known
before. I could see the woman in my mind, wearing a cotton
dress with a long, full skirt and a sunbonnet of the same
material, going down to the spring to fetch water for her
kitchen, stepping out of her way, now and then, to water
her roses, and beating down a path to them that remained
long after she had gone.

I liked this woman. She must have worked hard, for
there is much to be done on a new homestead. But she took
time out from her washing and cooking and sewing and
churning to plant flowers and tend them so well they could
still grow and spread their beauty long after the house had
decayed and become part of the earth that formed it.

I could see by the blazes that their land adjoined mine,
and I went there many times, as one goes to call on a neighbor. It was at twilight that I felt her presence most, for
this was the time when her day's work was done and when
she must have stolen the last of the daylight hours to work
among her flowers.

I made some new discovery each time I went. There was
an old orchard with gnarled crooked branches, ready to
flower when the sun shone warm on them. There would be
plums and peaches and little June apples for no one but the
birds and me to eat. And there was a large sugar maple that
must have been full-grown when the house stood there. A
swing surely hung once from its low branch, and beneath it
the ground was soft, where rooms could have been drawn
with a stick, for little girls to play at keeping house. There

were trees growing around it that had been saplings then, the kind little boys love to ride. Through the silence I seemed to hear the shouts of the children who once played here, and the song of the woman as she went about her work, and the call of "Gee" and "Haw" of the man plowing in the field.

The land now belonged to the lumber company. They were only interested in the tall, straight pines. The clearing, to them, was so much wasted land where the pines had not reseeded themselves. I did no wrong, I knew, when I dug up the burning bushes and lilacs for my own foundation plants, and when I thinned out the jonquils and the rose bushes to make another rose garden behind my house, leading out from the stone-paved patio. But, like the Cherokee that murmured an apology over the body of the deer he killed, I silently apologized for each plant that I took.

"After all," I said to myself, "the jonquils won't bloom if they are not thinned out once in a while. And the cows and mules kept the roses and lilacs so eaten down they had no chance to grow."

As one who keeps a canary or a dog for a neighbor who has gone away, I took her flowers and made a garden of my own with them.

Chapter V

ONE morning at dawn, when I was more asleep than awake, a bumble bee flew against the screen of my window and I could hear the hum of its wings in my dreams. The chickens, eager as always for their morning grain, had crawled under the fence of the chicken yard and were beneath the window, searching for worms and bugs, and singing contentedly to themselves. In my sleep it was like the drone of human voices in the room, and the bumble bee was like the entrance of one with great news to tell, whispering it excitedly to all who would stop to listen.

A feeling of loneliness came over me when I became fully awake, and stayed with me all day. As far as my eye could see, from both sides of the high ridge, there was only a mass of green tree tops, like a green sea rippling in the breeze. There were no open meadows and no houses with a feather of blue smoke reaching up to catch my eye. And there were no sounds that belonged to civilization, not even the whistle of a train nor the honk of an automobile, for the dirt highway was three miles away. I missed the sight of other people and the sound of friendly voices.

I was not alone. The woods, far as we were from the settlement in the valley, were full of wild animals, of deer and wolves, of wild cats, foxes, possums, coons, squirrels and rabbits, and the shy wild turkey. And with the coming of spring, there was life in the air about me, of wasps and bees and butterflies, and worms and bugs and little field mice crawled over the ground, hidden by the tall grass. A purple martin flew over my head and circled around the martin box on a tall pole that Rufus Wells had put up in the chicken yard, and a bright little blue bird, ignoring my presence, perched on the dead stalk of last autumn's goldenrod, swaying to and fro in the wind with as much enjoyment as a child in a swing. This activity was going on as if it were no affair of mine. I was an intruder, in the midst of all the life about me, something to be avoided or ignored as if I did not exist, or an enemy to be feared or attacked before I could make the first move, to be bitten, stung or hissed at. A blackbird flew over my head with a call that sounded as if he were laughing at me.

After the morning chores were over, when the chickens were fed and the cow was milked and the house made neat for the day, I went for a walk. It was time now to put in the vegetable garden and I must find someone to plow it. Last year, when I first came, I had planted a few seeds, but it was late August, and on new, unfenced ground, and even if the cows had not eaten it down, it would not have matured. But last year a garden did not mean the same, for now it meant life itself to me.

I walked toward the home of old Daddy Means. He had a plow and two jennies. I would have him get my land ready for the seeds. Dainty, pointed tracks in the road showed me that a deer had been there and had hurried away at my approach. Zozo sniffed at the tracks and ran, but she came upon the scent of a squirrel and followed that

instead until she came to it, perched high in a tree scolding
down at us.

Two lean mongrel dogs came out to bark at me from
Daddy Means' front yard, but when they saw my dog, they
came out to meet her, sniffing to become acquainted, then
romping happily together. The jennies grazed in the front
yard and smoke rose from the chimney of the little one-
room shack that was the old man's home. He was somewhere around, I knew, for his dogs and donkeys were there,
and a fresh log had recently been added to his fire. But
there was only silence when I called, except the romping of
the dogs and the jennies munching, and a faraway tinkle of
cow bells. I called again, and still there was no answer.

The house was so small it might have been a toy house,
the kind Hansel and Gretel would come across in the woods.
A long pole held it up where it had leaned with the wind.
I did not go inside, but from the door I could see a cot piled
with quilts, crowded between the two walls, one homemade
chair and table of rough pine lumber, and iron pots on the
hearth with wild game stewing in them. The odor reached
me where I stood.

Behind the house there was a cave, made to store potatoes,
cut in the slope of a hill, with a closed door on it. As I
turned to go away I thought I heard a noise in there, but
when I stopped to listen, there was silence again. If he were
hidden there, I decided, I would go away and leave him in
his solitude. But first I wrote a note on the back of an old
envelope which I had in my pocket. A low wind blew close
to the earth, causing the last year's leaves to dance, and the
grass moved as if I were walking on something alive.

At the path that led from the gate to my house, I saw the

footprints of bare feet that went one way, and of old shoes with flapping soles that had come and gone. Zozo felt somebody's presence in the house for she stood where she was, with her body stiff, and sniffed the air. Then she ran ahead to investigate.

When I went inside, out of the strong sunlight into the room, I saw in the corner near the hearth the shadowy figure of a young girl, sitting on the edge of a cushioned chair, with her dark eyes turned toward mine.

"Hello," I said.

"Howdy," she replied, hesitating as if she were not sure whether to get up or remain as she was. "I'm Savannah Massery."

"Yes. I remember you. I'm glad to see you again." It was good to hear a youthful voice at Rocky Crossing. "Didn't someone come with you, though?"

I looked around for the wearer of the shoes with flapping soles, for I knew that no young girl of the mountains goes walking in the woods alone, no matter how bright the sun is shining.

"Yes'm. Granny came with me, but she was bound to get back before sundown so she didn't stay."

I drew fresh, cool water from the well and squeezed in lemons and added sugar, and I put a plate of molasses cookies on a table between us. I was warm from my walk and I knew this girl, who had walked even a greater distance, would want refreshments. Her lemonade went down in one gulp. She hesitated shyly before taking the first cookie, but when I urged it on her and put the plate closer, they disappeared, one after the other. She did not eat and drink as a glutton would, but as one who has not seen food for a long time.

"Everybody calls me Vannie," she said, by way of conversation.

Her eyes were fastened on me as I sipped my lemonade. There was something else she wanted to say, I knew, and I tried to draw it from her. I asked about the people in the valley. They were all well. Uncle George Nixon had shot her father's mule because it had jumped his orchard fence and broken down his young fruit trees, but he paid Jeff Massery well for it.

"Time and again he'd told Papa to keep the mule out of his orchard," she said. "But the old mule wouldn't stay away. Yesterday, then, Uncle George came over and said, 'Jeff, I shot that—'" here she hesitated, then went on, for Uncle George's talk was sprinkled with *damns* and *hells* which she could not bring herself to repeat. "He said, 'Jeff, I shot that mule of yours. Here's a hundred dollars. Go buy yourself another one, but—but if that one gets in my orchard, I'll blow the—the thing to blazes, too.'"

A hundred dollars was a great deal to pay for the poor, bony mule that had hauled sand from the creek bottom to my home site. I knew Jeff Massery would not spend it all on another one. He would buy one as poor and sorry as the last, and there would be money left. But I also knew, as well as his daughter, that the money would not last long, and again he would be going to Uncle George for credit for a little flour and lard.

The girl wore her long hair pushed back behind her ears, and her dress, faded from blue to dingy grey, came halfway between her knees and her ankles. She tucked her bare feet, dusty from the long walk, under the chair, as if she were ashamed of them. I tried to read in her dark eyes her reason for coming. It was not merely to pay a call, for if it were, her grandmother would not have left her to go home alone.

Zozo ran to the door and barked, and then she wagged her tail. We heard the rumbling sound of a wagon approaching, and soon the crunching of feet on the path. It was old Daddy Means, with his two mongrel dogs trotting after. His two jennies, hitched to the gate, waited patiently.

He gave me back the note I had written on the back of an old envelope.

"You'll have to tell me what's in it," he said. "I don't know how to read or write."

"I'm sorry," I said. "I forgot. I wanted you to plow my garden for me."

He hesitated and I thought he meant to refuse. Then he said, slowly, "Now if that's not the beatenest thing you ever saw, as a fellow says. I was just saying to myself, 'I reckon I'll go and offer to plow that garden on the new homestead' and I brought my plow and harrow in the wagon with me. Now that's funny."

We could hear his calls to the little jennies as the earth turned under the plow. The cow came up to the calf lot with a motherly call and the calf answered, impatient for his milk. I started for the milk pail, and Vannie took it from me. I realized then what an amateur milker I had been. No wonder the calf was growing so fat. He was getting all the cream. I let Vannie strain the milk while I went out to the chicken house with a basket. At least the hens needed no help in giving me eggs. The pig came squealing to meet me and I had to feed her first, then I threw grain to the hens. A black snake crawled hurriedly out of my way, and I saw three suspicious lumps under his skin the size of eggs, undigested. I gathered the remaining ones he had left, leaving one that was marked, in each nest for nest eggs. When I returned to the kitchen, Vannie was waiting there for me, with the milk she had strained, cooling in a crock placed in a cedar bucket with freshly drawn water in it.

Now, as a hesitant swimmer who suddenly decides to plunge into a cold pool, she spoke.

"I come to stay and work for you."

She must have prepared a little speech in her mind, which she could not say, for she seemed dissatisfied with this blunt statement. My own thoughts were quicker than my words. I had no money to pay her. There was less than seventy dollars left. I must pay Daddy Means for plowing, and I must live, somehow, until the seeds I had planted could sprout and grow and bear. But she spoke before I had a chance to reply.

"I don't want money. All I want is some learning, and some shoes, and something to eat."

"The school in the valley," I started. "It's not far from where you live."

The school was open only five months a year, three months in winter between the last harvest and the first planting, and two months in summer when the crops were laid by. But Mr. James, the teacher, was conscientious. He tried to crowd a whole year's course in that time, to children from a tall, gawky boy of nineteen to the little four-year-old Wells child, seated together in one small room.

Then it came out. The little ones at school had laughed at her and the older ones felt sorry for her. She took cornbread in her lunch pail instead of flour biscuits, and when the children passed around their food for each to take a bite, no one bit from hers. And in the winter, when the ground was frosty or covered with snow, they looked down at her bare feet and pitied her. It had been their pity more than their laughter that kept her away.

Daddy Means came to the door.

"Come see what you think of the garden now," he said.

I went out to the freshly turned earth, harrowed and ready now for planting. I thanked him for the good job he had done, and when I went in for my purse, he called me back.

"Neighbors don't take money for doing neighborly things," he said, and he put his plow and disc in the wagon to drive away.

Urging the money on him had done no good. He flatly refused as if it were an insult. How could I return such neighborly acts, I wondered, to Daddy Means for plowing for me, to Rufus Wells for building the chicken house and to Jock Wheeler for building the fences and giving me the hen with the baby chickens, and to Uncle George who tried to keep it secret when the check I gave him came back from the bank?

I turned back to the house, where Vannie was puzzling over the oil stove in the kitchen. I showed her how to make the flame, and I started to prepare the evening meal.

"The dining room can be your room," I said. "We can move that couch from the living room, and one of the bureaus from the bedroom and we'll put the table by the south window and have our meals in the living room, or here in the kitchen in the breakfast nook."

Again there was a crunching sound on the path, and we saw old Daddy Means coming back.

"I wonder if I can borrow a little flour from you," he said. I looked around for something to put it in.

"I don't want much. Just a little," he said. "You can wrap it up in that old paper. That'll do."

I asked him to stay and have supper with us, but he went on his way. When he was out of sight, I lit the lamp and put it on the kitchen table. We sat in the pew-like benches at the breakfast nook, that were stained a deep pine color, with red muslin cushions on the seats. The girl watched every move of my hand, the way I held my fork, the way I buttered my bread, and the way I took the cup when I drank my chocolate. And because she imitated me, doing all the things as I did them, I was more conscious of my table manners than I ever was in all my life.

When the meal was over and the dishes were washed and put away, I brought out the mail-order catalog. We turned the pages to the young girls' dresses and we looked to see how they were made. I could afford only to buy the material and make them myself. I ordered cotton prints and ginghams for every day and three yards of pale-blue muslin for something to feel dressed up in. Then we drew an outline on a piece of paper for a pair of white and brown oxfords to fit her. And while we were waiting for the goods to arrive by mail, there were some dresses of mine that could be taken up temporarily on the sides and at the hem, for the girl had no other dress than the long, faded garment she wore when she came.

Chapter VI

THE frogs came out twice. We could hear their clear call from the creek and from the narrows. Then the north wind blew and frost returned and silenced them. The buckeye buds, like tiny green mittens, closed tight against it, and the earthworms crawled back into their holes. The birds stopped their glad songs and sat huddled against the wind, calling out feebly now and then in protest, and the snakes, stirring with new life in the sun, went back to finish their winter sleep. For the third time the frogs sang in chorus, from the shrill chirp of the tree toad to the deep bass of the bull frog. And a turkey buzzard circled over the chicken house. This meant that spring was really here, and it was time to put in the hardy vegetables.

We dug long furrows with our hoes, and we put in the pea and cabbage seeds, the onion sets and the slices of potatoes with their three eyes in. Vannie taught me to plant the things that grow under the ground, in the dark of the moon, and when the moon was full, to plant the things that ripen above. That was no harder to believe than the fact that these small, dry seeds dropped and buried in the ground would ever become tall plants and furnish us our food for the year. It was like the miracle of changing water into wine, or feeding the loaves and fishes to the multitude. Anything is possible to one who works on the land.

When the mourning dove cooed and the whippoorwill called at twilight, we knew there would be no more frost. It was safe to put in the tender vegetables, the beans and corn and tomatoes. We studied the patent medicine almanac Uncle George had given us for the right signs of the zodiac. Twin days were good for growing anything. But peas and beans planted on flower-pot day would only blossom and not bear fruit. That was the day we must plant our flowers. The best day of all, of course, was Good Friday, for the seeds planted then stirred with life and were ready to rise from the dark earth in three days.

Early every morning we went out to the garden to see what had taken place while we slept. We saw the plants slowly rise from the ground like little green-clad soldiers, in long, even rows. And the flowering weeds growing beside them were the gay camp followers.

"Don't chop that down! That's the little pansy violet," Vannie called out to me one morning when I was weeding the garden.

She dropped her hoe and stooped down to cover the roots I had exposed.

"They are so little, they won't hurt the onions," she went on.

The sweet Williams were in bloom and we left them as they were.

"Now that's the black-eyed Susy," Vannie said, pointing to a cluster of weeds sprouting among the potato plants. "They'll make pretty flowers when the sweet William's gone."

We didn't cut down the poke weed, for the tender young leaves gave us food that was as good as any vegetable we could grow in the garden. The chickweed was not really a weed, but a dainty white flower. So it was with all green things that came up from the ground. In the end we left everything except the deadly nightshade whose berries would poison, and the beggar lice whose burrs stick to our clothes when we go near them. We pulled up the oak and hickory shoots, too, that sprang from stumps cut down that would not die.

In the house, Vannie's eyes might follow me, silently learning how to hold her fork and how to put her clothes neatly in the bureau drawers and to keep her bed made. I was on my good behavior then, knowing that she looked upon me as the master and upon herself as the disciple. But in the garden and in the woods, it was I who learned from her. She saw every fresh track on the road that passed our house.

"A fat old coon came by here on his way to the creek," she said. "See how deep the tracks sink in."

"An owl caught a rabbit here. The poor little rabbit tried to get away, but the owl got him just the same," she said another time.

Once she found the nest of a rabbit, with three naked little ones in a bed of fur and grass, and she watched it every day to see that no harm came to them.

There was not a plant in the woods that she did not know by sight, though their names often puzzled her. I called the plant she had known as Indian turnip, a Jack-in-the-pulpit, and she was pleased. That was a much better name, she thought. She liked the name swamp lily for the lizard's tail.

The wild coreopsis was known to her as scurvy weed, and
she had me repeat coreopsis over and over until she learned
it, for she liked it better. But some of the names I taught her
she would not accept. Spiderwort was not a pretty name for
the little blue flower that closes up at night and opens
brightly in the sun. It was still the blue-eyed Mary to her,
and Indian pinks were the red star flower.

Some of the flowers had two names, hers and mine. The
hepaticas were the wind flowers and the cinquefoil, the
water strawberries. But some had no name at all, and we
gave them names of our own. It was a pleasanter way of
learning about Nature, from Vannie, than to go about with
a book in my hand, even though we did not know all the
names of the things that grew and the creatures that crawled
and flew about us. The yellow-spiked flower whose name I
still do not know, I call the moonbeam, and the New Jersey
tea, which I learned about later, will always be snowdrift
to me. And I do not feel guilty, for I can quote Walt Whit-
man, who wrote, "You must not know too much, or be too
precise or scientific about birds and trees and flowers and
water craft; a certain free margin, and even vagueness—
perhaps ignorance, credulity—helps your enjoyment of these
things, and of the sentiment of feathered, wooded, river or
marine Nature generally."

Vannie's vocabulary was rich in words and expressions I
would find hard to do without. I do not know of a better
way to say "I pleasured myself," or "We were only prank-
ing." But her ears were alert for the way I talked. If I did
not use a certain word, it must be the wrong word to use.
She gave up "ain't," because I did not say it. But she also

gave up using the word "clever" for "friendly" or "hospitable," until I learned to use it, too.

When the days grew warm, we took our clothes down to the creek to wash them, where the water was clear and soft. We waded out from the banks, with our skirts pinned high about us, and stood in the shade of the button willows, where the trees leaned far out from the bank. It was good to see towels and sheets and underwear turn white as we rubbed. When God said to Adam, "In the sweat of thy face shalt thou eat bread," I know it was meant as a blessing and not a curse. We felt no curse upon us then. Vannie always sang as she worked, and no matter what song she started, she always ended with:

> Amazing grace, how sweet the sound
> That saved a wretch like me.
> I once was lost, but now I'm found.
> Was blind, but now I see.

It was her favorite song. She loved the elisions, and she put them on every other word, swinging her voice up in a flute-like note. Zozo romped about the bank, and often Adolphus, the pig, came trotting with us and rolled contentedly in the mud at the water's edge.

When we were through, we took off the clothes that we wore, and washed them, too, and spread them with the others on low-growing bushes to dry. Then we lathered soap on our hair and over our bodies, and bathed and swam. Little schools of minnows came up in curiosity, and nibbled at our legs. We kicked at them and they swam furiously away, only to return again. Dragon flies hovered about,

swooping down to skim the surface where soap bubbles
floated, then they soared up again. And now and then we
could see a rainbow trout or a bass through the clear water,
swimming past us.

We watched the procession of life going along the water's
edge, a frog coming down to the water, an army of ants going off in a long line as if to war, a furry brown tarantula
crawling out of its hole in a hollow stump. Every minute
there was a small drama enacted before our eyes, but we
could not stay to see the end. The clothes on the bushes
dried in the sun smelling sweet of sunshine and we must
gather them in our arms and take them home to be ironed,
without ever knowing which side won in the battle of ants,
how the frog laid her eggs in the water, or where the
tarantula went for its walk. It was like starting to read a
book and putting it aside before we reached the end.

Wild azaleas and irises bloomed along the bank of the
creek, and when our bundle was not too heavy, we dug them
up and took them home to plant in the border of our rose
garden.

I told Vannie of the abandoned homestead I had discovered.

"That's the old Lewis homeplace," she said.

I wanted to know more about it, but she could not tell
me any more. Mr. Lewis had died and Mrs. Lewis moved
to Little Rock with the children long ago, and no one had
heard from her since. The wilderness has a way of drawing
a curtain over itself to shut out all who leave it, and to enclose all who had come here. There were few letters sent
from Uncle George's post office, and few were received, and
there was little contact with the world outside.

Except in the early spring when it was time to buy seeds for planting, and in the late fall when crops had been harvested and were taken to market, we seldom saw a wagon on the road to Rocky Crossing. We were safe bathing in the creek, even where the trail crossed it, for wagons and light footsteps could be heard from a great enough distance so that we had time to scramble to the bushes for our clothes and put them on.

Once we heard the footsteps of a donkey, and we knew that Daddy Means was on his way. We dressed quickly before he came in sight, riding bareback on the jenny.

"Seems like I smelt a dead man when I was here this morning," he said as calmly as if he were discussing a thing that happened every day.

He used the creek water for drinking and cooking, I knew, but running water purifies itself quickly, and our washing could do no harm to the water. But I thought this was his way of keeping the creek solely for himself, and I was annoyed.

"You just imagined it," I said.

"No, I didn't. I know what I smelt."

"Maybe it was a dead calf, or a little fawn," Vannie put in.

"It wasn't, either. It was a dead man. I ought to know. I've smelt dead men in the water before, and there's not another smell like it. You'd know that if you'd ever smelt it yourself."

We took our clothes home and thought no more about it. After all, the cows waded out in the water to drink, and so did the mules, and the deer and other creatures of the woods. The creek did not belong to him alone, and I would not be frightened away with such tales.

Wash day was the busiest day in the week, for we tried
to do all the inside work in one day. We baked and ironed
and scrubbed and dusted, so the rest of the week we could
do what we wanted.

I put the dough for bread on to rise before we went down
to the creek. And when we returned, I punched it down to
rise again. While Savannah ironed the clothes, I made
ginger cookies, custard pie, crackers of butter and salt and
flour, pricked with a fork to keep them from puffing, and
noodles of eggs and salt and flour, rolled as thin as tissue
paper and cut in strips to dry. A cheesecloth bag with the
whey of clabbered milk dripping through hung over the
table, on those days, to make our cottage cheese.

Vannie walked to and fro, from the ironing board to the
stove, putting down a cool iron to take up a hot one. She
paused in her song to test the iron with a wet finger, and
when it hissed like an angry cat, she sang on:

> Through many dangers, toils and snares
> I have already come.
> 'Tis grace that brought me safe this far
> And grace will lead me home.

The pile of clean clothes, neatly pressed and folded, grew
larger on the table of the breakfast nook, and the rolls of
sprinkled ones gradually disappeared. And on the long table
by the west window there were plates of cookies and crackers and noodles, and loaves of warm bread, fresh from the
oven. We stopped to eat luncheon in a busy, crowded
kitchen, of warm bread and rich, yellow butter, and cottage
cheese with thick cream. Then we scrubbed the kitchen

floor and swept and dusted the other rooms, making the house tidy enough to last another week.

Even on these days we stopped in the early afternoon. Sometimes we had to hurry to get through in time, and sometimes there was work left over for another day. But, like the Englishman who dresses for dinner in the jungle, we took sponge baths and changed our clothes for fresh, clean ones, and we felt like different people as we sat down to the afternoon lesson.

Vannie could not see the sense of so much washing at first. But habits are easy to form, and it was not long before she began going to the washroom of her own accord, when the long finger of sunlight coming through the south door had moved far over to the east.

There was a table with a bowl and pitcher in the washroom, and a secondhand bathtub where a hole was cut in the floor to let the water drain through to the lilacs and burning bushes planted around the foundation. We took showers by pouring water from a pitcher over our bodies, then lathering with soap and pouring over fresh water for rinsing. I drew the water for the pitchers while Vannie bathed, and she filled the pitchers for the next day, when I was through.

I had tried the orthodox way of teaching Savannah, remembering the lessons of my own childhood. But I soon learned I must invent a new way of teaching this girl of fifteen, who did not know whether the earth was round or square, who had never read the story of Cinderella and the fairy godmother, and to whom the name of George Washington was unknown. She could read and write and do a little figuring, and that was all.

The art of story telling was not lost in the mountains, nor
was the art of listening. I turned to the style of old Jock
Wheeler, and Vannie learned American history in the form
of stories as he would have told them. I told of the early
settlers coming to this country, as Jock Wheeler would tell
about his grandpappy, the first white settler in the valley,
who had come when the Indian nation was not far away.
But Jock's grandpappy had only wolves and panthers and
bears to worry about, for the Indians were quiet and subdued, then. I told of Indian attacks, also, and I told of the
wars with the French, and then the English, as Jock told of
feuds, where each side hated and killed for a cause he believed to be right. I tried to make the people who lived
then real to her, as real as the ones she knew down in the
valley. And when I told her about Europe, I thought of
Donald Houston, who lived beyond the valley. He had been
drafted in the war of 1917, and sent to France, a raw, mountain youth who had never been outside his settlement before.
When he came back, he had many an interesting tale to
tell, and he was still telling them.

There was no other way to work arithmetic problems except the one way of adding and multiplying and subtracting
on a piece of paper. Vannie did not like this as well as she
did her reading, writing and spelling lesson which we made
in one when she read from a book I had with me there,
W. H. Hudson's *A Little Boy Lost.*

She read aloud, one page at a time. That was her reading
lesson. All the words she did not know, she wrote down,
with the definitions I gave her; that was the way she learned
to spell.

I had not had time to think about Daddy Means' words

on the day he told us he had smelled a dead man in the creek, until we sat quietly down to the lessons. Now I found my mind wandering while Vannie read.

After what had happened, Martin could never visit the waterside and look at the great birds wading and swimming without a feeling that was like a sudden coldness in the blood of his veins.

I was only vaguely aware of her voice, slow and hesitating. How did a dead man smell, I wondered. There were many odors in the woods, and I had grown more sensitive to them since I came here. There was the smell of earth after a rainy day, the smell of growing things in the early spring, of wild flowers mingling, of pine needles in the heat, and of animals that had just left a spot we came upon.

I told Vannie the meaning of the words she did not know.

"Veins. Veins are the little tubes that carry blood to your heart. You can see them here in your wrist."

I looked on while she scrawled it out on the paper. Then I read aloud the words she had written down, and she spelled them out for me.

Now that I thought about it, there had been a different smell that morning. But I had thought it was the wild azalea that had finished blooming. My mind went back to the odor of flowers over a coffin in a closed room. Do we smell like faded flowers when we die, I wondered.

Vannie took her tablet and pencil and the copy of *A Little Boy Lost* back to her room.

"It was down in the narrows, where the creek turns the bend, that the screech owl called last night," she said.

I knew she had been thinking of death, too, during the lesson hours.

"Daddy Means doesn't want us to use the creek for washing," I said. "He was trying to frighten us. But after all, we are as clean as the cows that stand there to drink. We'll go on using it as we've been doing."

The brindle cow left the herd she had been grazing with, and came back with a full bag, bawling on the way to let the calf know she was coming. There were little impatient replies. We took down the milk pail and the basket for gathering eggs, and went out to do the evening chores, and we forgot about dead men's smells.

Chapter VII

ON THE following Saturday we went down to the valley for our mail and supplies. Once a week we took the long walk of ten miles each way, and we had to get up at dawn to make our preparations.

While Vannie did the outside chores, I tidied the house and prepared the supper so there would be nothing to do but warm it over when we returned. We drew the water for our baths and put out a change of clothes, and I spread the prettiest embroidered cloth on the tea table in the living room and set it with the best china and the silver teapot. After the long climb home, we wanted a touch of luxury and daintiness for our tired bodies.

We started out when the sun was just showing over the tree tops. Under our arms we carried empty burlap bags to bring back the supplies, and the mail that had been accumulating for a week. We had a lunch of sandwiches and cookies, with a few extra ones for little Ona Massery. We knew she would get them all, as she always did, for at every house that we passed along the way we were greeted with, "Better come on in and stay for dinner."

Zozo trotted ahead of us, holding her tail high and her nose close to the ground. Now and then she followed some fresh scent in the woods, but she soon came back, wagging her long, bushy tail happily when she saw us, as if she had been gone a long time. I was glad I had not allowed her tail to be cut, for she was as proud as a peacock of it.

Before we reached the big road, I heard a noise of broken twigs and little mincing steps behind me, and I turned around to see Adolphus running toward us on her dainty feet, like a Chinese lady of old. We tried to chase her back, but it was no use. She went for a little way, then when we started off again, she came trotting after. I had been determined not to grow fond of her. I had told myself she was only so many hams and bacons and buckets of lard to me. But in her loneliness, she insisted upon making herself a pet, and she was determined to follow wherever we went. We gave up and went on our way, with the dog sniffing at fresh tracks in front of us and the pig behind digging furrows in the ground in the hope of finding an acorn or a hickory nut, and grunting happily.

We came at last to the blacksmith shop of Rufus Wells. It was a pleasant place to stop and rest, with upturned logs the height of chairs, to sit upon, and the walls hung with pieces of old iron to be made into hinges or pokers or wagon rims, and horseshoes turned up to hold luck. I liked it best when he was busy, shoeing a mule or putting a rim on a wagon wheel, with a bright fire burning under a hooded chimney and the anvil ringing pleasantly. But now there were other men gathered there, some from beyond the valley that I did not know well, and I did not go in. Rufus Wells looked up and smiled, and I waved in reply and went to his house on the hill where I found Lizzie Wells on the porch churning. There is a code in the mountains that

women do not go where there are only men around. I kept
the code, but sometimes I did so reluctantly, for I liked to
hear the tales men told of hunting and trapping and of
strange, supernatural things that happened to someone they
once knew.

"Come on up," Lizzie said, bringing out chairs for us
from the kitchen.

When we were seated, she went back to her churning and
said nothing more. This silence annoyed me when I first
met Lizzie Wells. I had thought of it as rudeness. But when
I came to know her, I found a certain comfort in it. She had
no small talk. Even her oldest friends in the valley, and the
members of her own family, had heard little more than
monosyllables from her except when she had something
important to say. But her face could light up with a smile
that took me in and made me her friend. We sat sometimes
for hours, with neither of us speaking, and we did not feel
ill at ease, for we had no need for words.

She sat with her profile to me as she churned. It was like
those I had seen in old Dutch paintings. Her house had a
Dutch quality, too, with its floors and furniture scrubbed
so with sand and ashes that the wood still kept its bright
color after years of wear.

A baby lay on a quilt spread on the floor of the dog run,
and a little girl with yellow hair was playing with him. He
was more interested in the mystery of his pink toes, and he
held them up for us to share that mystery with him. A barefoot boy came out of the kitchen with a piece of cornbread
in his hand, and he ran down the hill to the blacksmith
shop. There was no loud talk or laughter from the men

now, as there usually was when they gathered together. They were strangely quiet, with only the low murmur of their voices reaching us.

Rufus Wells came striding up the hill to be with us, and I asked him to cut my hair. It was growing long and hard to manage, and now was the time to cut it, for I had seen the thin sliver of a new moon last night, rising over the hill beyond the narrows. Rufus had the sharpest scissors and he cut all the hair in the valley. He brought out a chair with no back for me to sit on, and Lizzie put a flour sack around my neck to catch the falling hair. I wondered why Rufus was so serious as he clipped away, but I asked no questions. He would tell me in his own time if he wanted me to know. I asked about their oldest son, working his way through school at the county seat, and he gave me the news, saying he would return in the summer.

"I want my hair cut, too," Savannah announced.

"No, Vannie. Once it's cut, it's so hard to grow back again. It's pretty the way you wear it now," I said.

It brought back my own childhood to see her comb it out and braid it in long pigtails. But for all the shy look in her eyes, she was stubborn.

"I want it like yours," she insisted.

I shook my head and Rufus called out in protest.

"Now you made me cut that side too short. I've got to cut all the rest to match it."

Vannie had her way in the end. There was a picture of a girl in the mail order catalog, the one wearing the dress we planned to copy, when the material came. She wanted to look like that. When Rufus had finished with me, she sat on the stool and put the flour sack around her neck.

"Guess you heard about that man disappearing at Gordon Hâle's place," Rufus said.

"No. Nobody's passed along the Rocky Crossing road for several days except old Daddy Means, and I haven't heard any news at all," I answered.

"Don't know his name—somebody working around there. Just disappeared, but his wife and young one are still around."

Lizzie lifted the churn dasher and yellow balls of butter clung to it. She went into the kitchen for a bowl and a wooden spoon to dish it up.

I thought of Gordon Hale. There was an air of mystery about him and his farm. I had seen him only once, when he came to dig my well and worked just one day. The men who lived on his place were never seen. They took no part in the affairs of the valley, the church meetings, the play parties, sitting up with the sick, or the burials. Having them close to us but not a part of us was like having some dark, ugly thought in the back of our mind, which we could not put away.

The baby on the pallet began to cry and I picked him up to rock him in my arms, but that was no substitute for the milk he wanted. His mother took him and gave him her breast, and I worked the butter for her. Vannie stood up and looked in the mirror hanging on the outside wall. The short hair made her look older, but she was pleased with what she saw. Zozo, patiently waiting on the ground, sprang up when she saw us start down the steps, but Adolphus was nowhere to be seen. We searched and called, but there was no answering grunt. Secretly I hoped she was lost, for I was beginning to wonder if we could ever bring ourselves to kill her for her hams and bacons.

"Better just stay on here till dinner time and eat with us," Lizzie said.

We replied that we must be on our way, and Rufus went out to join the men in the blacksmith shop. There were men gathered at the post office, too, but unlike a blacksmith shop, women could go there even when there were only men present. They were talking about the man at Gordon Hale's and my ears were listening, though I must pretend to be thinking only of the mail.

"The little girl saw it. The man's own daughter. She saw it with her own eyes, I tell you, and told the Smith girl about it," one of the men was saying.

"Shot him down in cold blood with the woman and the girl looking on, then wrapped barbed wire around him and threw him in the creek when the water was high," the man named Smith joined in.

I could feel a cold wind blow over me and I thought of what Daddy Means had told us.

"Why don't you go on home now," I said, turning to Vannie. "I'll join you there later when I get the mail."

But Vannie's ears were taking in everything she heard, and she refused to leave.

"Well, you can't prove a man's been killed without you see the body," Uncle George said. "What good will it do to fetch the Sheriff unless you got the body to show the man's been killed?"

"But he threw it in the creek when the water was high. In reason the body's been washed clear to the Mississippi by now."

"The man's gone. That ought to be proof enough. And the woman's living on with Gordon Hale."

"That's no proof, I tell you. A man can go away and leave his woman and young one behind. That's no sign he's dead."

"Judge not, lest you be judged," Jock Wheeler quoted.

"Is there any mail for me?" I asked Uncle George.

"Hell, yes. I'll be obliged to build on to the post office to hold all the mail you've been getting," he replied.

He went to the pigeonhole and brought out the letters. "Two here from New York. One from San Francisco. One from Memphis addressed on a typewriter and one that looks like it's from your folks."

Uncle George liked to hear me read my letters aloud, to know the news that was happening outside. Even with this murder mystery in our midst, he waited expectantly while I opened the mail. He had come to know my family and my friends through their letters. He called them by their first names, as I did, and wanted to know if Zula had bought her house yet, and if Georgia ever married that boy she was in love with.

"Any news about the war?" Jock Wheeler wanted to know.

Japan had gone into Manchukuo, and President Hoover had protested. By the time the news reached our settlement, the rumor had grown to a war between America and China, for everything beyond the Pacific was China here.

The trouble had passed over, I could say, and I read bits from the letters that would interest my listeners. I was like a wayside traveler or a wandering minstrel, bringing news from countries far away.

There were two large packages waiting for us, one from

Sears, Roebuck, with Vannie's shoes and material to make her clothes, and there were magazines my father had sent me. I needed flour and corn meal. That, with the packages, was enough to take up the hill on our backs. The feed I had intended getting for Adolphus would have to wait another week.

We went to the rooms back of the store to visit a while with the womenfolks. Mrs. Nixon and her two grown daughters were in the kitchen canning poke greens. They had been listening to the talk of the men. Now and then the youngest girl went to the door to hear better, and came back to repeat what they had said.

"That girl down there's always telling things whenever she finds anybody that'll listen to her," the older daughter said. "I came across her once when I was picking huckleberries, and she told me she'd seen a bear just then and it stood in her path and she couldn't go home. Wanted me to go with her."

Mrs. Nixon set extra plates on the table for us and insisted that we sit down to eat with them.

"A body'd think there wasn't a thing to eat in the whole valley, with you bringing your lunch that way," she said.

It was a breach of etiquette for a mountain woman to sit at the table when company was there. She must remain standing, ready to bring hot cornbread or biscuits from the oven, and to fill the glasses and cups with milk and coffee when they were empty. It was only when everyone was through that Mrs. Nixon sat down. I lingered on and sat with her while she ate, but I have never learned whether it was the right or wrong thing to do. My own manners were not up to the mountain standard, for when the wagons from the valley passed down the Rocky Crossing road, and the people in them stopped to have a meal with me, I liked to sit with my guests and join in their talk.

I helped wash the dishes and put them away, and we took our leave, saying we would stop again for our bundles on our way home. We went on to the Massery house, where little Ona came running out to greet us, stretching eager hands for the sandwiches and cookies we brought. It was like watching a hungry little puppy eat, when she tried to put everything in her mouth at once. Vannie held the child up in her arms, and I felt a sudden desire to take them both back with me when I saw the affection between the two sisters. I wondered if Mag, sitting listlessly in the squalor of her surroundings, had any feeling for her children other than the maternal instinct all animal mothers have. The grandmother came into the room then, and when I saw her stirring about the room, with her bright eyes taking in everything, I knew the force that had held them together.

Granny Massery wanted to know about the murder, and Vannie went into every detail, adding even a little more from her own imagination. I saw how legends grow, with something added at each telling.

If I had secretly rejoiced because Adolphus was lost, it did not last longer than the day. When we reached home after a steep, steady climb of ten miles, we saw her round, black form, mincing down the road in the twilight, to meet us. The chickens flew down from their perch and followed us to the door of the house, and the cow stood by the calf lot, pretending she did not notice us while the calf was struggling to put his little black muzzle between the fence rails to steal the milk.

I turned the cow in the lot with the calf. Let him have the feast alone. We were too tired to milk that night. Then I fed Adolphus and closed the gate of her pen while Vannie scattered grain for the chickens and brought in the eggs. We put the Southern spoon bread, mixed that morning, in the oven to bake while we bathed and changed our clothes. I had made over two old evening dresses I knew I would never wear again, for nights such as this. If a stranger had happened to come then to this log cabin in the wilderness, he would have thought us crazy, dressed in old party dresses while we sat at the tea table before the fire and ate our dinner of spoon bread and poke greens mixed with scrambled eggs, and drank our tea from Limoges cups set on an embroidered linen cloth. But we needed the feel of soft silk and thin china and linen, after a twenty-mile hike down hill and up again, with a load of thirty pounds on our backs the hardest half of the way.

When the table was cleared, we lit the lamps and opened our packages. I read my letters again, enjoying them more in private, and I turned to the magazine before me. My father has sometimes regretted he had let his life slip by without accumulating money to leave to his children. But he has given me a heritage that is worth more to me than all the money a man can earn, for I inherited a love of reading from him. I was like one standing before a table piled with food and not knowing what to take first. I glanced through one magazine after another, starting an article here and a story there, but I could not concentrate just yet, for my mind was skipping ahead to the others yet to be read. Later, when I was relaxed, they would be read slowly through, even down to the last advertisement.

Savannah tried on her new shoes, and she said they were a perfect fit. Even if they were not, she would never let them go, to wait days without any until they could be exchanged. And she held the material for dresses against her body and looked in the mirror to see the effect.

"Tomorrow's Sunday," she said in a wistful voice. "I reckon it'd be wrong to sew on Sunday."

"There's nothing that says we can't cut on Sunday," I answered. "We'll lay the patterns and cut the cloth tomorrow."

Cutting dresses and panties and nightgowns and slips would take the whole day. Early Monday morning, we could start to sew.

Chapter VIII

O UR garden grew. First there were green onions and radishes, and lettuce leaves, then there were new potatoes, peas and string beans. The corn was tall and tassels began to form, and the squash and pumpkins were vining, covered with yellow blossoms where bumble bees flew in and out. Food grew along the roadside, too, poke greens, heartweed and cinquefoil, and dewberries were ripening under the dry oak leaves. The weeds grew, too, and all the wild flowers we had allowed to come up with the vegetables. We hoed around them and between them, and we gathered their blossoms and brought them to the house, so that all indoors was like a garden. Every bowl and vase was filled with wild petunias, New Jersey tea or snowdrift, as Vannie called it, black-eyed Susans and blue-eyed Marys, and even the horsemint, with its innocent, starry look and its rank smell.

It was a time of growing. The little Carolina wrens and orchard orioles were growing too large for their nests, and they were testing their wings, to fly away. Already their parents were singing of another wooing and another brood. Adolphus was getting fatter each day, demanding more and more food, and the hens hid their nests in the woods, like quails, concealed in the brush, and they came up later with flocks of baby chicks. The rabbits, in the nest that Vannie had discovered, grew, too, and looked upon our garden as their own. Zozo thought of them as so many barnyard animals, and quietly let them come.

I tied her in the garden one night, thinking her presence there, at least, would keep the rabbits away. But there came a violent thunderstorm, with lightning flashing and thunder roaring, and rain beating down heavily. I awoke and went out in my nightgown to bring her in, and I saw her long, bushy tail drooped in shame for the only time in her life. She had been punished, she thought, but she did not know why. From then on, the rabbits shared the garden equally with us.

The wagons that had passed our road earlier in the season on the way to town to buy seed and new farming equipment, no longer came now. It was a busy time in the valley. The men worked from sun to sun, cultivating their fields of corn, sorghum, sweet and Irish potatoes and whippoorwill peas, to put away for their winter food. Each farm had a cotton field, too. This thin, mountain soil was not intended for cotton. It took five acres to raise a bale, but it was a cash crop, and the money it brought bought shoes and overalls and dress goods, and flour, sugar and coal oil for the year.

The land was the only boss these people knew, and it was a stern, hard master. It must have all a man's daylight hours, and it paid what it would. Sometimes, if there were a flood or drouth, or insects and disease, a man had nothing for his year's work. But there were none who did not love this master, and love the work, too, no matter how tired he was at the end of the day of harrowing and hoeing in the hot sun. None, that is, except thin, yellow Jeff Massery, who

shook half the year with malaria chills. Work, to him, was
something to be despised and avoided whenever possible.
This was an election year, and the county had our little
dirt highway graded and paved with gravel in the low,
muddy places. Jeff left his young crop to grow in weeds, and
worked for a while on the road. But when it became tire-
some, he quit that, too. The money he earned went the
way of the money Uncle George gave him for the mule, a
little here and a little there, and soon there was nothing
to show for it. Granny did what she could, but her body
moved slowly. She could only work in the vegetable patch,
with what help she could get from Mag.

The women of the valley worked as hard as the men, adding to the cooking and washing and looking after the children, the care of vegetables planted close to the house. They
brought out their empty fruit jars and scalded them and put
them on fence pickets to be sterilized by the sun, ready to
hold food for the winter.

I had bought new fruit jars when I first came. Now I took
them out and put them, empty, on the pantry shelves. Every
day we shelled peas and snapped beans and every day a few
of the jars were filled. Then the blackberries ripened in the
clearing that had once been the field of the old Lewis
homeplace. We went out with our tin lard buckets to gather
them for canning, and we found Daddy Means always there.
We each claimed the patch as our own, and no matter how
early we were, there he was, picking as fast as he could. It
came to be a race to see who could get there first, and pick
the most, and he always won.

"I know another place over in the burnt woods where
there's a blackberry patch," Vannie said one day when we

had gone at dawn, leaving unwashed dishes and unmade beds, and an unmilked cow, only to find him there before us.

"Then we'll go to the burnt woods tomorrow," I said.

Early the next morning we went down to the narrows and up again to the burnt woods, and there was Daddy Means, picking fast away. He gathered the berries to sell to Uncle George for the things he needed that he could not raise. And we were gathering them for our winter food. It became a game to us which each tried hard to win, to see who could gather more berries.

The cow learned to wait for the milking. She came later in the morning to her calf, and the hens laid their eggs without their early grain. Zozo went with us and fought the yellow jackets nesting in the grass beneath the berries, but Adolphus was getting fat and lazy as she grew older, and preferred to lie in the shade of her own pen. Besides, she had a companion now. There was one chicken left in a brood that was hatched in a secret place in the woods, and I took it from the mother hen, because I needed her for laying. The chicken was pecked and abused by the others in the chicken yard, and it took to going to the pig pen adjoining, eating the food Adolphus dropped from her trough, and perching on her back to sleep at night. It followed the pig wherever she went during the day. Adolphus apparently paid no attention to the chicken, but she must have been pleased with its company, for she no longer insisted on being with us.

We gathered berries early in the morning and cooked them and put them in jars when we returned home. Sometimes a family from the valley came up to join us, and we did our gathering together, canning, then, at the berry field, over an open fire. They came back home with us to have supper and spend the night, to get an early start for picking the next day. We spread pallets on the floor for the children to sleep upon, and we sat up late, boasting a little over how much we had done, and how many jars we had already canned. The Wells came and the Wheelers, and once Mag and Granny Massery walked up with their buckets. We gathered that day for them and helped them put it up to take back home.

In the beginning it had been fun, but after two weeks I had had enough.

"We've plenty of berries put up now," I said, looking at the rows of deep red jars in the pantry.

"But there's still some mellowing in the burnt woods," Vannie said. "Daddy Means will get them if we don't."

That was a challenge which she knew I could not refuse. But when the sun beat down on me and the briars scratched and the chiggers and ticks leaped from the grass and leaves to make a feast of me, I wondered why I should go to such lengths for a little food. The next morning I was firm. Was I not a woman grown? Must I take orders from a child?

"We won't go today, Savannah," I said. "We've more berries put away now than we can possibly eat. There's work to be done about the house and we'll stay at home and do it."

Vannie worked faster that day than I ever saw her work before. When we brought the clean clothes back from the creek, she had them ironed and had started dusting and scrubbing before I could make the dough for baking. I was still working in the kitchen when she washed the floor around me. I wondered where such energy came from. Certainly not from her father, nor from her mother, whose indifference was equal to the father's laziness. It could only have come from Granny Massery, with a sparkle in her black eyes that could still dance though her body moved slowly. They told it in the valley that she had been wild in her youth. It was even whispered that Jeff was not his father's child.

"I'm through now," Vannie said when it was still early in the afternoon. "I'll just go over yonder and pick the mellow ones before time for my lesson."

She put me to shame. There was nothing I could do but take up my bucket and follow. We were alone in the burnt woods, for even Daddy Means had had enough of picking berries. There was a song of birds around us and the hum of yellow jackets trying to drive us away from their nests. We heard the call of a red bird, and a bob white and the staccato notes of a woodpecker. Surely a whole flock was near, singing together, each one taking up where the other left off. But when we looked up, we saw a mocking bird, alone on a bough of a large sweetgum imitating all the sounds he had heard. He flitted his long tail as if he enjoyed the joke he had played on us, and he flew away, singing as he soared. Blood dripped from our legs and arms as we went back home with our buckets full. We poured salt over our wounds to kill the chiggers and ticks, and we took pitcher baths and put on fresh clothes. It was time now for the chores of evening, and for supper. We must wait till lamplight for the lessons.

The supper was cooking on the stove when I heard the rumbling sound of a wagon coming down the road. Hastily we peeled more potatoes and shelled more peas, and I cut

extra pieces of gingerbread and whipped another cup of
cream to put over them, for a wagon passing on this road
always meant company for us. Ours was a halfway house,
with no other neighbor except Daddy Means for six miles
on either side. Whoever passed, whether strangers or those
we knew, stopped here to rest and water their mules, and
to have a meal and visit with us. I had come to know what
real hospitality was. It was sharing from a scanty supply of
food, piling quilts on the floor for beds, and giving up all
privacy. But it meant, too, laughter and talk and a friendship bound closer with each visit. There was not a home in
the valley or in a stranger's home beyond where I would
not be welcome and they were welcome here.

The rumbling sound came closer. We could hear the
mules stepping on the rough road and the talk of young
children, and we waited at the open door to greet them.

"It's a queer time of day to be starting out anywhere,"
Vannie said.

We wondered who it could be, for the sun was far down
in the western sky, throwing shadows longer than the trees
themselves on the ground. At last the wagon came in sight.
It was piled high with household furniture, pulled by two
lean mules, tugging and struggling with the load. A man
and woman and a young girl sat on the seat in front. The
woman and the girl each had a baby at her breast. In the
back, crowded in with the furniture were several small,
fair-haired children, and a young boy walked beside the
wagon with two young girls, all in their bare feet.

"It's the Longs," Vannie whispered to me.

Now I held my breath, for fear they should stop. I had
heard about these people. They lived far beyond the valley,

near the county line, but they were close enough so that their lives touched ours. The three young girls and the boy were children of the old couple, and the little ones were children of the old man and his daughters. Some even said that the baby at the woman's breast was the child of her son, but others said it wasn't so, that she was a long-suffering soul, who had stood for things no woman should be expected to bear.

In the city there can be good and evil all around you, but it does not affect you because you don't know it is there. Here, isolated as we were from others, the sins of our neighbors became our sins, too, and the good they did we made our own. Uncle George's generosity became ours, and it helped form our own character, and so it was with the courage of Granny Massery and the goodness of Rufus Wells. Even Jeff Massery's laziness we could accept, because he was not a well man. But the unpleasant mystery about Gordon Hale and the people on his place, and the evil we knew of the Longs, made us feel guilty, as if it were, in some way, our guilt too.

"Howdy," the old man called out.

"Howdy," I replied.

They came to the gate and then passed on, and I gave a sigh of relief. A chubby little girl, as fair as an angel, waved her hand, and I waved in reply, and they drove on until they were lost to sight, around the bend in the road. They brought a note of discord in their passing that lingered with us after they had gone.

The sun went down and the clouds flared red, like a bed of hot ashes fanned by the wind. A soft gold light settled on the grass and the leaves of the trees, and on the road where the wagon had passed, and the wind blew gently as if to sweep the world clean again. It brought the fresh smell of wild roses and pine to us. The grasshoppers took up their evening song to the setting sun, starting low and rising in one long, wavering crescendo, and the katydids joined in like a tambourine accompaniment, with the shrill chirp of crickets in the grass. A dove cooed and a red bird called out sleepily. High in a dead sycamore an eagle perched and looked the landscape over, then it flew away to its nest, and when we looked closely down the hill toward the narrows, we saw the bushes move as some wild animal pushed them aside on its way to lick the salty earth. It was as if a dark cloud had passed over us and was gone. We turned back to our supper, feeling clean again.

Chapter IX

THE days were hot and still, and the hills disappeared behind a haze of heat as if a thin curtain had been lowered over them. Twice the cardinals and mocking birds and Carolina wrens had courted and brooded and raised their young, and now they were courting again, singing from tree to tree all day. In the evening the insects took up where they left off, and the song repeated itself in our minds over and over as a monotonous tune will do.

There is something about the languor of summer, the hot, indolent days with a heady perfume of pine and grass, that fills us with an unknown longing such as spring, with its clear, crisp air, can never do. Everything was touched with the same voluptuous beauty, the lush, green foliage with the seed pods opening and blowing in the wind, the sleepy, soft murmur of wild bees carrying pollen from one blossom to another, and the mating call of a bird with the sweet, shy answer from a near-by tree. We were close to these things, yet not quite a part of them.

Vannie had her fifteenth birthday. Sometimes she had seemed like a little old lady to me, with her knowledge of things I did not know. She was so serious as she went about her tasks that I teased her and called her Miss Vannie. She knew instinctively where the huckleberries were ripening and she warned me to gather only the she-huckleberries, for the he-huckleberries were poison. She told me, too, which plants were known for their cures, the wild coreopsis, or the scurvy weed roots made into a tea was a cure for scurvy, and the swamp lily was good for a poultice for boils. Mullein roots, she said, mixed with hickory bark was sure to cure a cold. She told me which barks and roots could ease a woman's pain in child bearing, and which would bring about an abortion.

There were times, too, when she was like a little child, learning from me the things she wanted to know.

"What for do we call the calf Cinderella?" she asked.

"Because we get the best of the milk and give him what we don't want," I answered.

Still she did not understand, and I told her the story of Cinderella. She had heard legends and old ballads, handed down from one generation to another, but she had never heard a fairy tale before, and she listened with the eagerness of a child.

Vannie wore one of the new dresses for her birthday, but not her best one, the pale-blue batiste with dainty ruffles at the neck and sleeves. That one she was saving for some special occasion, and she did not wear her shoes. She had been ashamed of her feet when she had no shoes, and kept them hidden as best she could under the chairs and tables. But now that there was a new pair put away in tissue paper, she did not mind her bare feet any more.

I had baked a birthday cake and I was experimenting with substitutes for candles. Small new tips of pine branches, so like candles when they are on the tree, were pretty with their pale green against the white frosting. But they would not burn. They only smouldered and died. I put a match beside each pine bud. The matches would give the flame and the pine buds would give the beauty. The cake might taste of pine and sulphur, but it was the girl's first birthday cake and I wanted it to be as pretty as a birthday cake should be.

"We'll have it this afternoon," I said, leaving it on the kitchen table. "When the lessons are over, we'll have lemonade and birthday cake."

A wagon came down the road and stopped at the gate, and a woman got out, followed by six boys. The oldest was about twelve, and the others had followed in such quick succession that they were like stair steps, all looking alike with yellow hair and blue overalls and bare feet. It was the Widow Johnson who lived a few miles beyond the valley. She came to the gatherings there and I had met her before, but her home was so far away I had never visited her.

"Come in," I called, going out to meet her.

"We're on our way to the county seat and we stopped for a drink of water," she said, taking the chair I offered her.

The two oldest boys went out to draw water from the well. They took some in a tub to the mules that waited by the gate, and they drew another bucket for us. The younger boys went with them, and each time they passed through the kitchen they stared at the birthday cake and its green pine trimmings with wistful eyes. They were clean, healthy boys. Their father had died soon after the birth of the youngest, and the mother was raising them singlehanded. She was as strict as ever a father would be, so it was said.

Each one had his work to do, even down to the least one. Some helped her plant and harvest in the fields and some helped with the cooking and washing.

Now, she said, she was taking the boys to the county seat to hear a lecture in the high school there by a college president from near Little Rock.

"He was born up around Faulkner County where I came from," she said. "I want my boys to see him and hear him, so they will know how high a man from these woods can go if he has a mind to."

We talked of those who had gone out in the world and made good, and we talked of those who had stayed behind, and made good. And surely that too, we decided, was important.

Then woman-like, our conversation drifted to our own work. We talked about our gardens and how we needed rain, and about the canning we had done. Mrs. Johnson still had jars of food left from other summers.

"I've never reached the bottom of the food I've canned," she said, proudly.

I showed her the jars of the first canning I had ever done, and we went out to look at the garden where the vegetables I planned to put up were beginning to ripen.

Before we went I put a plate of molasses cookies on the kitchen table for the boys. When we returned, not only were the cookies gone, but the birthday cake had been eaten, too, with only the matches and pine buds left strewn about the table. The youngest one, Virgil, looked up at me and smiled. His chubby cheeks and fists were smeared with white icing, and there was a glint of mischief in his eyes.

What consternation I felt, I quickly hid, but Vannie was

not so successful. Mrs. Johnson's face did not change expression.

"I reckon we'd best be on our way," she said, quietly.

"But you've only just come," I protested. "It's close to dinner time. Stay and have dinner with us."

No amount of coaxing could persuade her.

"We've a long trip ahead and we'd best be going," she said with decision.

She climbed up on the seat of the wagon and took up the reins and drove off. I learned afterward, from Daddy Means who saw it, that she stopped the wagon when she crossed the creek, and got out, calling the boys after her. She whipped them every one, from the oldest down to little Virgil, then she had them get back in. Once more she took up the reins and drove on her way.

Within a week she returned, and stopped at our gate. It was a hot, lazy day. The bees and wasps filled the air with their humming, and the katydids called at noon. Even the wind was not cool. It blew softly, like a warm caress, making slow, sensuous music in the pines. Vannie saw the wagon from her window.

"It's the Widow Johnson and those young ones," she said and she drew the monk's cloth curtains over the open doorway so she would not be seen.

The widow left her six sons in the wagon. She came down the path with a tall young man, dressed in town clothes instead of overalls. His hair was dark and it had a slight curl, with a lock that kept falling over his forehead, and his eyes were blue.

"This is Alan, my sister's boy," the Widow Johnson said, by way of introduction.

"Pleased to meet you," he said, extending his hand.

He had that kind of sophistication that comes from living in crowded places. There is something about brushing shoulders with strangers on the sidewalk that makes a man feel superior to another who lives in the woods alone.

"Have you come here to live with your aunt?" I asked him when we were seated.

"No. I'll just stay a little while. Thought I'd start a singing class here," he replied.

"We used to have singing school every year back in the old days," Mrs. Johnson put in. "But it's been a right smart while since we've had one now." Then she turned to her nephew. "Sing some, Alan. Let the folks hear how you sing."

"Yes, do," I joined.

"I've got no voice for singing," Alan protested, modestly.

"Yes, he has, too. He's just saying that. My sister says he's every bit as good as the ones that sing over the radio. Go on, Alan. Sing."

Though he lived in a town that was the county seat, there were mountain settlements only a few miles away in any direction, and he must have heard the songs of the mountain people. But when he sang for us, it was nothing more than an imitation of radio hillbilly music as I remembered it. He sang about a man taking leave of his sweetheart, to go off to prison for twenty-one years. And at the end of each stanza he yodeled, as the radio cowboy singers do.

The monk's cloth curtains over the doorway leading to Vannie's room parted and she came in to join us. She had put on her shoes, and her new blue dress with the ruffles on the neck and sleeves. Her eyes were turned toward Alan, but

when he looked at her, she blushed and turned shyly away.
He smiled and went on with his singing to the end.

It's raining, it's pouring.
The sun never shines.
Twenty-one years, babe,
Is a mighty long time.

Then there was a lusty yodel.

"That was the way the radio singers do it," I said when he
was through, and I could not have given him a better com-
pliment.

The boys in the wagon were restless and I could hear little
Virgil crying for his mother. Mrs. Johnson arose to go.

"Let them come in," I pleaded with her. "Stay and have
dinner before you go down the hill."

"No," the Widow Johnson said firmly. "I told those boys
they couldn't come in this house again. I raised them up
better than to act like a passel of hungry wolf cubs when
they go a-visiting."

"But cakes are easy to make. I'm glad they had it and
enjoyed it."

"That's not it. I'm raising them without a father and I aim
to do it right."

Vannie did not stand at the door to watch them depart.
Could it be, I wondered, because of the superstition that a
young girl who watches her sweetheart out of sight will
never see him again?

Though I had looked upon Vannie as a little old lady,
with a wisdom greater than mine in many things, or as a
child with so much yet to learn, I had not seen her before

as she really was, a young girl just entering womanhood. She had the body of a healthy child when I first saw her. Now I realized that, even in the few months she had been with me, the soft curves of a woman were beginning to form.

In the days that followed, she stood long before the mirror to stare at her reflection. She rolled up her hair at night to make it curl, and tried new ways to fix it. She kept her dresses clean and her shoes were out of the tissue paper, ready to put on at a moment's notice. In her eyes there was a look of expectancy and her ears were ever listening for the sound of someone coming.

She bent mullein stalks toward the direction of the valley and she watched to see if they would die or rise again. When they rose, it meant someone loved her, who lived down there. No spider could build a web above our door. She watched carefully and brushed each one away, for if it were left there, it was a sign he would not come again. When the first star of evening appeared in the sky, or a red bird flew toward her, she stood where she was with her lips moving, silently making a wish.

Once we heard footsteps approach and Zozo ran out to bark. Vannie rushed to her room and put on her prettiest dress. And Bill Wells, the oldest son of Rufus, came down the path and asked for a drink of water.

I was glad to see him, for I was fond of the boy. He had his father's deep-set grey eyes and he had the same blunt hands that could make things. He drew fresh water and when he had drunk, he followed us indoors. I asked him to stay on for supper, and I sat with him while he ate. Vannie kept the code of the mountains, a little humiliated at my own lack of manners, and stood in the kitchen, waiting until he had finished, before sitting down to her own meal.

"Now you've only one more year to go," I said.

"Not exactly," he replied. "I've a year yet at high school, but I aim to go on to college."

"How?"

"I've found out about places where a poor boy can work his way through. I mean to see which one is the best and go there."

As he spoke, he turned toward Vannie, dressed in her pale-blue batiste with ruffles. Here was something he had not expected, his eyes plainly said, that little ragamuffin of a Massery girl suddenly grown into a lovely woman.

If he had only come a little earlier, Savannah might have met those glances with some encouragement. The languid summer heat and her fifteenth birthday, with the knowledge that she had now become a woman, made her ready for her first love. Alan was the first to come along, and I could see she was now fiercely determined there would be no other.

After Bill Wells left, I praised him to Vannie.

"He's a fine boy," I said. "And he'll go far in the world."

She agreed with me, but when we spoke of him, her voice was not the same as when we mentioned Alan.

Vannie kept her thoughts to herself and she did not confide in anyone, except when we went to the creek to wash our clothes and to bathe. There was something about the creek that made us feel closer, and we talked of things that we might have kept secret in any other place. The name of Alan came often to Vannie's lips then, and she grasped at every chance to bring him into our talk.

"Just think, when I saw those Johnson boys coming in the wagon, I was still so plagued about the birthday cake I like not to have come out at all. I was fixing to go out and pick huckleberries and not come back till they had left. Just think how near I came to that."

"You would have met Alan in time," I answered. "He's staying a while with his aunt to start a singing class in the valley. You'd have been sure to run across him at some time or other."

It must be lonesome for a young girl here on the mountain ridge, I thought. I went back in my mind to my own first love, to the thrilling ring of the telephone, the parties and the new party dress, movies and tall ice-cream sodas and a stolen kiss under the mistletoe. But I was older than fifteen then. Fifteen is still the age of a child, I told myself.

"Vannie," I said, "do you want to go down to the valley and stay with your folks a while?"

She looked up quickly, as if she were a little hurt.

"It pleases me more to live here," she answered.

I thought of Ruth and Naomi, and I said no more. The water lilies were in bloom. Vannie picked a yellow blossom and put it in her hair with a bobby pin, then she looked down at her reflection in the water and smiled. A school of minnows swam by and the ripples they made distorted her smile into a grimace. She began to sing, but not her favorite song, *Amazing Grace*. Instead I heard the words,

It's raining, it's pouring.
The sun never shines.
Twenty-one years, babe,
Is a mighty long time.

Vannie was no child at fifteen.

I found my own ears listening for footsteps on the road, and my own eyes looking eagerly out the window every time the dog barked. But when Alan came, it was when we were least expecting him. We had been gathering huckleberries that grew beyond the rose garden, and we were in the kitchen canning them when we heard a voice call, "Hello."

Vannie dropped the big preserving spoon and hastened to her room. She drew the curtains close, while I went out, hot and perspiring, with stains of huckleberry juice on my apron. I invited him in, and scarcely had we sat down when Vannie appeared from her room, as if she always wore her best clothes in the morning, with shoes on her feet and a flower in her hair. But a shyness came over her, and she could think of nothing to say.

I left them alone. It is a thing that is never done in the mountains, but I broke the code for the canning must be finished. The door leading from the kitchen to the living room was open and I could hear their voices, Alan's confident talk and Vannie's shy answers. He stayed until after the noon meal, and again she would not watch him go on his way.

There was a new sparkle in her eyes now, the kind that still lingered in the dark eyes of her grandmother.

"When is he going to start the singing school?" I asked.

"He's changed his mind about it. Said he's going to Little Rock and sing over the radio and be like Bob Burns and Lum and Abner."

I had not heard of Bob Burns or Lum and Abner then.

No one in our valley had a radio, and I had not listened to one for over a year.

"Who are they?" I asked.

"I don't know. He just said he was going to be like Lum and Abner and Bob Burns and I was too hacked to ask him who they were."

Chapter X

THE drouth that year was like a burning fever over the earth. Week followed week, and no rain came. The grass blades and leaves reached out thirstily in the early morning for dew that did not fall, then they drooped, wincing in the hot sun. Like Chinese coolies we drew bucket after bucket of water from the well, and poured it in trenches close to the plants. At first we watered the roses and wild irises too, but when the well ran low we thought only of saving the vegetables that meant life to us. In spite of the water, they wilted in the intense heat. A few small tomatoes bravely ripened and blistered but no blossoms formed, and flowers fell off the pole beans without fruiting as if they had been planted on flower pot day. The flowering weeds we had allowed to grow, absorbed what moisture they could from the soil and mocked us with their sturdiness. There was nothing now to gather from the garden except the black-eyed Susans and the chickweed, so we had flowers enough but little food.

The creek was like a lean, hungry animal, sprawled lazily on the ground, scarcely moving, with its white rocks like gaunt bones showing. Every day we looked up to the sky, but it was cloudless, and at night the stars shone piercingly. Vega was like a bright lantern which we might reach out and touch with our hands. But the stars were not beautiful to us now. We wanted to see them through a film of clouds.

The birds no longer sang. They went about with their little beaks open and their wings spread away from their bodies. Even the bobwhite and the mourning dove were silent, and long ago the frogs had given up their nightly serenade.

Only the insects flourished in the dry heat. They hummed and mated, and reproduced their own kind on every plant in the garden. We sprayed and pinched off eggs and crushed worms under our feet, trying to save the little wilted vegetables until the rain could come again.

I have seen nothing in my life uglier than two squash bugs mating. We pulled them off the leaves, still joined together, and stepped on them, shuddering in disgust.

Too much life had been created, and we had to become murderers merely to live. Often we saw a black snake coiled in a nest in the hen house, with the eggs he had swallowed, bulging from his side. We could count them, sometimes one and sometimes many, when he stretched up to stick out his tongue at us. We killed the snakes with hoes and sticks, and hung them on a high branch of a tree as a warning to other snakes.

I needed a small boy about the place who didn't mind killing things, I had said in the early spring when I had to drown a pretty field mouse and her three downy little ones who had made a nest in my linen closet. A boy was the last thing I had expected to appear, then. But in the late summer, he came.

Bob came quietly into our lives. Even Zozo had not barked when he walked down the road in the late evening. I was digging a trench in the baked earth between the tomato rows when I heard a voice speaking to me. I turned around and saw him looking over the picket fence as if he had appeared, like a genie, out of vapor.

"Do you need a man to work for you?" he asked in a voice that had been forced low.

I was too surprised, seeing him there, to answer right away.

"I'll make you a handy man," he went on. "I'll cut your firewood for you and I can hunt and fish for your meat."

Vannie had come soon after the failure of the bank had left me with nothing but the few dollars that happened to be in the house. Now, with the hot sun scorching the garden that must supply us with food, here was another, asking for a home. I could not take in anyone else. But it was growing late and the nearest house to mine was far away. I could not let him go without inviting him in for a drink of cool water and a meal.

"Come on in," I said.

He disappeared and came around to the garden gate. Then I saw, standing before me, a child no more than twelve years old, with about as much dirt as can crowd on one small person. He had been standing on a rock to appear tall, and even now he forced his voice to a lower pitch, to pretend he was older. There was a strong odor about him of unwashed clothes and skin. I sent Vannie to the house for a cake of soap and a towel and a pair of clean pajamas.

"You've enough time before supper to go down to the creek and bathe," I said. "Take off your clothes and we'll wash them for you."

He went behind a large pine and stripped off his trousers

and shirt. He left them on the ground, so thick with dirt they were stiff, and ran toward the creek waving the pajamas and towel like a banner. While the supper was cooking, Vannie and I heated water in the iron wash pot behind the rose garden, and sprinkled lye in it to boil the clothes.

"Do you know who he is?" I asked Vannie.

"Seems like I ought to, and yet again I can't remember him," she replied.

It took several scrubbings before the boy was finally clean, but there was a great improvement even when he came back from his first washing in the creek, with the pajamas rolled up at the knees and the sleeves flapping over his hands. We sat down to our supper at the breakfast nook in the kitchen, and his voice was now the natural voice of a small boy.

"What is your name?" I asked.

"Bob Jenkins."

Vannie gave a start of recognition then, but she said nothing more. She sat at the table with us, for she had evidently not looked upon this child as company to be waited upon.

"Where are your folks?" I went on.

A grown man coming to this place would not be questioned. Who he was and why he came was his own affair. But when a child came asking me for a home, there were things I wanted to know. The boy did not answer me.

"Bob," I asked, "where are you from?"

"I just come from California," he replied.

I looked at him in astonishment. California was more than two thousand miles away. What could the child be doing here?

"Are your folks out there?"

He hesitated again.

"I ain't got no folks," he said at last.

I had been reading in the papers, before I came here, of homeless waifs, victims of the depression, roaming over the country by the thousands. But this was not one of them, I knew. In the first place, his accent gave him away as one who belonged here in the mountains. And, too, we were thirty-five miles from a train and no automobiles came down the dirt highway that went through the valley unless there was a reason. Bob enjoyed being the center of attraction with all eyes turned toward him, taking in all that he said.

"I didn't like it out there. I didn't even stay there a day. Went there yesterday and came back today."

Vannie turned to me. Her face was serious but her eyes laughed, for she had studied geography enough now to know that California was three days and three nights away on a fast train.

"California's far," was all she said.

"Sure it's far. That's why I didn't get here till near dark," Bob answered.

I asked no more questions, for I knew the boy would tell only what he wanted me to believe until he could trust me enough to tell the truth. His clothes were still wet on the line, so we made up the folding cot and put it in the kitchen. After breakfast, the next morning, I would send him on his way.

Vannie and I sat in the living room, reading, after he had gone to bed. He blew out the kitchen lamp and we heard him settle on the cot.

"I know who he is," Vannie said softly to me. "He's that

old man Jenkins' boy. The old man didn't have a wife. She took sick and died and he was drunk after that all the time."

"Were there any more children?" I asked.

"Yes. Another boy and a girl. The Widow Johnson took the girl and kept her till she got married and left. But the boys wouldn't let anybody do for them. They used to steal from other folks' smoke houses and gardens and they ate frogs and lizards and nobody could do a thing with them till the Sheriff came and took them off to Little Rock."

"About how old is Bob?" I asked.

Vannie counted. "I'd say he was about eleven or maybe twelve. I reckon he came back and found out his Papa was dead and he didn't have anywhere to go."

There was a sound like a stifled sob from the kitchen, and then silence. The boy could not have heard us, for we were talking in whispers, and sounds don't carry well through log walls. Again I heard a sob and I went to the kitchen door.

"Bob," I called gently.

There was no answer, but I knew by his breathing he was not asleep. The moon shone through the window, lighting his bed and leaving the rest of the room in shadow. I touched the boy's cheek and his tears wet my hand. He had talked so big and tried so hard to be a man during the day, but now he was only a little boy come back to the only place he could call home. I started to tiptoe out of the room, but he called me back.

"Don't leave," he pleaded.

"Bob," I asked, "why did you leave Little Rock? Weren't they kind to you there?"

He would not answer.

"Promise you won't send me back," he said, sitting up in bed.

"I can't promise until you tell me more."

"They were all right. Only—" he hesitated. "Only they don't keep a boy after he's grown up."

He was still not ready to trust me, so I asked no more about it then.

"Do you want to stay here with us?"

"Yes'm," he said eagerly. "I'll make a handy man around the place. I'll——"

"It won't be easy living here. They gave you good food and clothes at the orphanage and an education. And there were boys your own age to play with. You won't have that here."

"I don't care. I'm not going back. Nobody's going to make me go back. Besides, you promised."

"I haven't promised yet."

"If I tell you the truth, will you promise?"

"Yes."

"Promise first."

"I promise."

"Well, I didn't run away from the 'sylum. They turned me over to a dairyman and I ran away from him."

The moon shone on his face, lighting the streaks of dirt that he had not washed away, and on his blond, rumpled hair.

"Now you've already promised. You know what happens when you break a promise," he said.

I didn't know. There have been many who broke promises and nothing seems to have happened to them.

"I'll keep the promise I've made," I assured him. "You can stay on here and I won't let them take you away."

When he saw me start to turn away, he called me back again.

"Tell me a story," he said. "They used to tell us stories in Little Rock before we went to sleep."

I felt relieved, for no child has been mistreated who has bedtime stories told to him. Now the change was so complete from the swaggering little boy he was when he first came that I laughed and sat beside him on the cot.

"What kind of story?" I asked.

"No kid stuff. Something about men and boys."

I told him about Daniel Boone scouting in the wilderness, how he was captured by the Indians and how he escaped and found his way back to his fort. Vannie crept in, with her nightgown on, and sat on the cot with me to listen. She had never heard a bedtime story in her life. When I had Daniel Boone safe back at the fort, I lowered my voice and spoke softly, and I knew by the boy's breathing that he would soon be asleep.

Vannie tiptoed back to her room and I lay in my own bed while the moon rose high over the tops of the pines, and the dipper swung around on its handle. Figures were dancing in my head and would not let me sleep. There was fine timber on my land but I could not sell it until I had finished the homestead period and had title to the land. The little money that was left after the bank failed must be stretched to meet all our needs until then. We had to buy staple supplies and feed for the animals, kerosene for the lamps and matches and soap. And I had wanted to send off to the mail-order house for a jar of cold cream and a lipstick. It seemed foolish, even then, to be weighing cold cream and a lipstick against this child.

"But he was better off in the orphanage, with his orange juice and spinach and bedtime stories than Vannie ever was, or even the Widow Johnson's sons and his sister who had made her home with them," I told myself.

All my doubts of the night left me when morning came and I saw him playing with Zozo, still wearing the pajamas with the trousers and sleeves rolled up.

"She's nothing but a play dog," he said in disgust. "I saw a possum track as plain as day and I tried to make her follow it but all she'd do was wag her tail and jump on me."

I could hear Vannie singing in the kitchen. "It's raining, it's pouring. The sun never shines." The water in the kettle boiled and sang. I poured some in the pitcher and called Bob into the washroom, where I washed his face and neck myself. Then I washed his hair.

"Gosh! I washed good last night at the creek," he said. Then he screwed up his eyes and shouted, "Don't get those suds in my eyes."

"Twenty-one years, babe, is a mighty long time," reached us, even in the washroom.

Bob's hair and face were a few shades lighter when we sat down at the breakfast table.

"Don't we say our prayers before breakfast?" he asked.

I grew up at a time when it was smart to have no faith. We debunked everything and everybody. When we were through with all the heroes of history, we went on to God and the Saints. But even in my doubts, the most beautiful memory I had was of kneeling at my mother's knee, in a white cotton nightgown and my hair rolled up in rag curlers, repeating the Lord's Prayer and adding, "God Bless Mamma and Papa and Georgia and Abner and Zula." I lost something fine when I lost my belief in miracles, when I no longer thought that water could be turned to wine or Lazarus brought back from the dead.

It had been a long time since I had prayed. I turned to Vannie, but her eyes were like those of a child upon me. With two, now, looking to me for an example, I suddenly found it possible to turn again to the things I thought I had lost.

"Yes," I said to Bob. "We'll say our prayers before breakfast."

I knew of no better prayer than the Lord's Prayer, and when we sat down, we lowered our heads and said, "Our Father, which art in Heaven." Bob said the words with me, but Vannie, who did not know them, repeated them after us, line for line. Their faces were solemn as they sat with bowed heads, but when we said "Amen," they went back to their thoughts.

"I'm going to show her how to hunt and we'll have meat every day," Bob said.

"Show who how to hunt?" I asked.

"Zozo. I'm going to make a work dog out of her. A play dog's no good about a place."

A yellow butterfly came through a crack in the screen door.

"Somebody's coming wearing a yellow dress," Vannie said. "Or maybe a yellow shirt."

Chapter XI

A MOURNING dove called from the narrows in the early morning. Vannie said it meant we would go off in that direction. It was the day to go down for the mail, and I said, "Let's make it come true, then. Let's take a short cut through the woods and go that way."

It had always seemed a useless waste of energy to walk three miles to the main road and then bend east again with it. If we went due southwest down in the narrows and up again, we should come on the road close to Uncle George's post office.

"I'm not going," Bob declared. "I'll stay on here and look after the place."

I knew his reason for not wanting to go and I did not urge him. This was the only home he knew, but because he had stolen food from the people of the valley he had come to look upon them as his enemies. Vannie and I went on with our preparations. I wrapped some sandwiches and fried pies in a napkin and poured buttermilk in a fruit jar for our picnic lunch.

"We'll take the compass so we will know when we are going in the right direction," I said.

"Like Daniel Boone in the wilderness?" Bob asked.

"Yes. We'll have to be our own scouts."

Bob began to weaken, and in the end he came with us. "You didn't lock the door," he said when we left.

"Somebody might pass by while we are gone and want to rest and drink some water from the well," I replied.

Bob was the scout. I let him hold the compass and he blazed a trail for us by bending down stalks, Indian fashion. We were the settlers following him to the new land. But Vannie, in her pretty blue dress, carrying her shoes to put on just before she reached the valley, did not look the part. A rabbit ran ahead of us and hid behind a log.

"Pow! Pow!" Bob shouted. "I killed a bear!"

Then we saw a possum resting on the limb of a red oak, with its long tail wrapped around it. It was so still, and blended so with the grey of the trunk, that I would never have noticed it if Vannie had not pointed silently.

"Pow! Pow!" Bob shouted again. "I killed a panther!"

He turned to Zozo in disgust. "You're no hunting dog. You're nothing but a play dog." Zozo only wagged her tail contentedly.

When, in the narrows, we saw a doe and her fawn turn to stare at us, then run away at our approach, we stood still, breathlessly watching. Even Bob was touched by the beauty of their movement, like the flash of a graceful, rhythmic dance, and he forgot to point his imaginary gun.

Vannie pointed out the tracks in the ground and told us what animals had been there before us. A possum's tracks, spread out, led to a rotten log or a tree stump, a fox's tracks were farther apart than a dog's and in a single line, and a coon's toes pointed straight ahead.

From our house, the ridge behind us looked steep and near. But when we were there, we found ourselves in a deep forest with only a gradual incline. We made our own path, with the compass for our guide, winding in and out among the tall trees and the fallen logs. It was easy to believe, with Bob, that we were scouts in an unknown wilderness. At last we came upon a path and we followed it, for we thought it must surely lead to the road.

Sometimes it seemed that our compass jumped, and the sun slipped over to the other side of the sky, but we kept to the path. Perhaps it went an easier way, I reasoned, and avoided steep inclines. We had left early, before the sun had climbed high, but now it beat fiercely on us, even in the pine forest. A suspicion came over me that this was not a short cut, that we had chosen a longer way after all. I could not see the top of the ridge from where we were, for the land sloped gradually, but surely we were somewhere near, for we had been walking long.

At last we discovered what a true woodsman would have known all along. We had been following in the path of an old tornado. The trees that had fallen in its way, and their roots, had long ago rotted and become part of the earth, leaving small mounds here and there to show where they had been.

We sat down, with the realization that we were lost. The sun, directly over our heads, gave us no clue. Bob shouted "hello" and his voice repeated itself against the hill, but there was no other sound except the faint rustle of leaves where some startled animal ran away from the noise. Zozo might have found the way for us, but she was content to be wherever we were, so she curled up at our feet, undisturbed.

"I'm hungry," Bob said.

We spread the lunch on a rock. There was time enough

to worry about where we were, later. First we had our sandwiches of cream cheese and blackberry jelly, and hard-boiled eggs and pickles, and we drank buttermilk from the jar.

"We are still going uphill, so we haven't reached the top of the ridge yet," I said. "Give me the compass, Bob. We'll go southwest as we started out in the beginning. That's bound to take us to the valley."

The incline was so gradual that we scarcely knew when we reached the top and started down. At last we came to the creek again, that had wound through the narrows and around the hill. Across it we saw a cabin, with smoke rising from the lean-to kitchen.

"We'll go over and find out where we are," I said.

Vannie held back.

"The creek crosses the road a good two miles on yon side of Uncle George's post office," she said. "We'd best go back that way."

I had had enough of scouting through the woods. Even Bob had long ago given up his games of make-believe, shooting at wild Indians behind the trees or following the tracks of wolves and bears. He had even tried walking on his hands to make the tracks of a bear in the dirt, and he had tried to make Zozo walk with one foot directly in front of the other, to make the clean line of a fox's tracks. Now he was weary and lagged behind. I had my way and we crossed the creek. Bob took off his clothes and swam naked, with Zozo paddling beside him. Vannie and I waded, holding up our skirts. The water was high here, for it met the river close by, and the rocks we stepped on were sharp. We could not hold out our arms for balance, because I carried

Bob's clothes and Vannie the burlap bags and her shoes. More than once we slipped and almost fell, with the water rushing past us, eager now, to reach the river.

On the other side a dog came running to bark at us, growling wickedly between barks. Zozo ran to meet him, and after a few sniffs they were romping together as old friends. It was pleasant to hear farmyard sounds again, the crowing of a rooster and the bawling of a calf, and the clattering noise of guineas. Even the dog running out to bark at us had been a welcome sound after the suppressed wild sounds of the forest.

We called out when we approached the house and a woman, toothless, with thin hair stringing over her eyes, and a faded, dirty dress hanging loose from her bony shoulders came to the door. A little girl, equally dirty, stood beside her and stared without saying a word.

"We are lost," I said. "Can you tell us how to get to the highway?"

Unlike the other mountain women, she did not invite us in. She hesitated before she spoke. Then she pointed beyond the creek we had crossed.

"It's yon way," she said.

I heard a chirping sound from her bosom and I thought I must have been imagining things.

"How far is it to the post office from here?" I went on.

She hesitated again, and again there was a chirp from her breast.

"About three miles," she replied at last.

We were tired and I would have liked to sit down and drink cool water from a dipper, and rest a while. But there was something about the place that depressed me. It was the kind of place one comes to in a bad dream, though the house was like any other house in the valley, of rough, un- painted lumber, roofed with hand-rived shingles, and the calf and guineas and chickens were the same as barnyard animals anywhere. Again there was a chirp from the wom- an's bosom, and I saw the downy, yellow head of a chicken peep out from her dress. It was no doubt the only one that hatched in a nest, and she was keeping it away from the mother hen, hovering it beneath her dress as a hen would spread warm, dark wings over it. I had seen Mrs. Wheeler do the same and we had laughed together over it. But this was a woman I could not laugh with.

"Thank you," I said and started on my way.

She turned without a word further and went back in the house, followed by the child, and she closed the door behind her. On our way back to the creek we saw two men ap- proach us with guns. One was Gordon Hale and the other, slightly younger, looked very much like him.

"Howdy," they spoke when they came near.

"Howdy," I replied. "We lost our way trying to find a short cut through the woods to the post office, and find we've come much too far."

"It's nowhere near here," the younger man said.

"We're going that way a piece ourselves. You can come with us," Gordon Hale put in.

No man went out in these woods without his gun, I knew, for he might come across wild game which meant meat for his family. But the guns these men carried as one walked ahead of us and the other behind, made me feel un- comfortable. Bob did not take off his clothes to swim across the creek this time. He rolled up his trousers as far as they would go and held my hand while he waded. Even the dog, swimming before us and waiting on the opposite bank until we caught up, sensed something unpleasant and she looked anxiously in our eyes for the meaning.

In our walk, we came across the charred ruins of a house where a yellow cat was sitting, forlorn and alone. He arched his back when Zozo approached, but it did not take even a cat long to learn how harmless our dog really was. He came up then and rubbed against our legs and purred. I reached down to pick him up. We needed a cat to catch the field mice and rabbits on the place.

"It's bad luck to move a cat," Vannie said in a low voice.

"But it's bad luck for the cat when he's left behind," I replied, and I put the cat, squirming, in an empty burlap bag.

We were subdued in the presence of these men and we talked to each other in whispers. At the road, the men stopped.

"Now you go three miles up this road and you won't miss it," Gordon Hale said.

His voice was not unkind, and after he and the younger man turned back toward their home, we could believe they had accompanied us merely to show us the way. The feeling of depression left us. Even Zozo, who sensed our moods, trotted happily again, waving her tail. It was not possible, now, to think that this man who had walked with us had killed another man and thrown his body in the creek, for the sake of the toothless woman with the chicken chirping in her breast.

Vannie stopped to put on her shoes. Her blue dress, crisp and clean when she had started out in the morning, now clung to her, wet and bedraggled. She ran her fingers through her hair and patted it in place, and she bit her lips to make them red. I saw the reason, when we came to the Widow Johnson's place. But Alan was not there.

"Better come in and stay a while," the Widow Johnson called.

Bob walked on and would not let her see him, and Vannie was impatient to go on her way, since she did not see Alan with his aunt. I stopped to explain that we were late and must be on our way.

"Is that the Jenkins boy with you?" she asked.

"Yes."

"Well, I declare. How are you, son? I'm proud to see you back again."

Bob mumbled something and went on.

"His sister stayed on here with you, didn't she?" I asked.

"Yes, till she married that Tailor boy and went off to Ola to live."

"Is she still at Ola?"

"I couldn't say for sure. Folks leave here and we never hear again where they are nor what they are doing."

Vannie went on to her own house, but it was not long before she was with us again at the post office, with her blue dress hurriedly pressed. She tried to pretend not to be looking about her for a tall thin youth with black hair that curled. But Alan was not there, either. Daddy Means was the only one in the post office. He had sold some timber from his place and Uncle George was explaining the contract to him.

"Now you put your mark here," Uncle George said.

Daddy Means made the mark of a cross on the paper and Uncle George folded it and put it in a long envelope.

Bob stayed beside me and kept his head down, believing no one could see his face. He was no longer Daniel Boone, or a bear making tracks in the forest. Uncle George looked closely at him, but said nothing. Daddy Means offered to take any heavy load up the hill for me. I bought feed for the animals and corn meal, and he put it on the jenny's back and started off. That left an empty burlap bag to take the cat back home.

"Now I want two pairs of boys' overalls and a jumper," I said.

Uncle George looked at Bob again and brought out the overalls to fit him. I gave him the money and he gave me back some change.

"I thought overalls and jumpers were a dollar each," I said.

"That's for men's sizes. Boys' sizes are fifty cents."

"I don't believe it," I said. "Where's the price tag?"

"I don't mess up my goods with price tags. Hell, you know it don't take as much cloth to make pants for a boy as for a man."

He turned to Bob before I could question him more.

"Here, son, put a pair of these on now. By God, those breeches are tight enough to choke you."

Bob went behind the counter and put on the new overalls.

"Then give me an order blank for Sears, Roebuck," I said.

I could order the lipstick, at least. Sour cream might be a good substitute for cold cream, but I was not ready to use pokeberry juice for rouge. And I was not ready to grow old like that toothless woman we had just seen.

On our way home, the Wheelers called out to us, and Rufus and Lizzie Wells asked us to come in and stay a while, and Bob saw only friendliness in their eyes. He put his hand in his overalls pocket and a knife fell out.

"I found it! I found it!" he said before I had time to ask where it came from.

"It's Uncle George's knife," I said.

"But I found it. What you find is yours."

"Not if you can find the owner, Bob," I said. "We'll go back now and give it to Uncle George."

The cat began to squirm and struggle to get out of the bag. I argued with myself that I was being hard on the boy, that the knife could wait until we came again next week. But in the same breath I was arguing, too, that I was tired and the way back was long, and I would not listen to those arguments.

"You wait for us at the Wells', Vannie," I said.

There was no need to punish her for Bob's deed. She was tired, too, and she hesitated.

"No, I'll go back with you," she said.

We left the yellow cat in the bag and the clothes we had bought, with Bob's old ones, at Rufus Wells' blacksmith shop, and retraced our steps back to the post office. Alan was there, and the fatigue left Vannie's face.

"We found this knife and I believe it's yours," I said to Uncle George, feeling that Bob must look upon me as the meanest person alive.

"We didn't see you when we passed your aunt's house," Vannie was saying to Alan.

"No. I was over at Donald Houston's place."

He bought a chocolate bar and gave it to her. Uncle

George took out another one and gave it to Bob, who accepted it in surprise. This was not what he had expected would happen. He ate it at once, but Vannie kept hers tightly clasped in her hands, in spite of the heat, all the way home.

"Just think," she said, as we walked up the steep hill again, "I came so near to not going back to the post office again."

She spoke as if it had been divine guidance that led her tired feet back. Then there was doubt in her voice. Donald Houston was a widower who lived alone with his fifteen-year-old daughter, a few miles from the valley.

"Wonder what Alan was doing there at the Houston place?" she said.

Then again there was awe in her voice.

"Just think, I almost stayed on at Miss Lizzie's to wait for you."

Bob threw the wrapper of his chocolate bar away. He showed no remorse for what he had done. Taking the knife had evidently meant no more to him than breaking off a limb from a tree to use as a walking cane or hobby horse. But something seemed to puzzle him.

"Reckon Uncle George knows who I am?" he asked.

"Yes, I'm sure he did," I replied.

He was silent for a while, then he said, "Uncle George can say his prayers all right, I bet."

I knew what he meant and I nodded. If Uncle George's debts to God were forgiven as he forgave his debtors, the balance was on his side, in spite of his doubting and disbelief. And he could say, "Forgive us our debts as we forgive our debtors."

We let the cat out of the bag when we reached home. He roamed from room to room, silently snooping in all the corners, and sniffing at the bags of feed and corn meal Daddy Means had placed inside our door. At last, when his curiosity was satisfied and he had drunk his fill of the milk I poured for him, he curled up in a warm spot on the floor where the sun had been shining through the south door, and purred contentedly.

"That house where he came from," Vannie said. "That house that was burned. It must have been where the man lived that disappeared."

It had been on Gordon Hale's land, and now, I remembered, it looked as if it had only recently burned. New grass had not had time to grow over the old charred blades and the vine that lay sprawled on the ground seemed to have just lost its support. I looked down at the cat and he blinked his eyes and looked very wise. What secrets he knew, he would keep to himself.

Chapter XII

I LIVED in the poorest section of the state, and my state is one of the poorest in the Union. We were the bottom rail, the downtrodden and oppressed. We were the forgotten ones. But we were remembered in that year of the drouth, for that was election year. Men whose names we scarcely knew came to the valley in the oldest automobiles they could borrow. They wore working clothes, of khaki or blue denim, suspiciously new, that had never known the sweat and dirt that comes from plowed fields. They learned our names and talked to us familiarly, as if we had been the best of friends all our lives. They were one of us then and they made a cause of us which was their cause, too.

They held a rally at the churchyard at night and we brought out benches from the schoolroom to sit upon. Two oil lanterns hung from the branch of a post oak and the men stood, one at a time, on the bed of the wagon under the light, to talk to us. They praised themselves and they made vague promises and told us we were the salt of the earth. We listened. A little boy cried because he could not see, and his father took him up, on his lap. The baby in Lizzie Wells' arms grew restless and she opened her dress to give him her breast. Zozo romped with the two black dogs of Daddy Means over the mounds in the graveyard.

A large man climbed clumsily into the wagon and began to speak. Someone in the back barked like a dog, and another took it up. The dogs stopped in their play and barked, too, and there was laughter even among the women. We had understood little of what the other men had to say. They had talked vaguely of the things they planned to do. We had heard all that before, and it meant nothing to us. But here was something that touched home, something we did understand. This candidate had voted for a bill in the state legislature forbidding the hunting of deer with dogs. The barking sounds were meant for the protests of the dogs. The laughter, however, was good-natured for they were free men among us and they went on hunting when and how they chose.

When the speeches were over, we drank iced lemonade from paper cups. The children were given sticks of peppermint candy and the grownups were given poll tax receipts if they wanted them.

"Damn it all, no man alive's going to tell me how to vote," Uncle George said.

"Well, the way I figure it," Jeff Massery spoke in his quiet voice, "it's not in reason for a fellow to have to pay a dollar to get somebody else an easy, good-paying job. The one that wants the job ought to be the one to pay."

Yet on the day when the election was held in the little white schoolhouse on the hill, Jeff Massery, whose vote was bought, and Uncle George, who traveled on horseback the thirty-five miles to the county seat to pay his dollar, voted the same ticket.

Old Daddy Means came in and Donald Houston, who

counted the ballots, helped him check the names and he made his mark with a cross.

"What about this one?" he asked, pointing to the space for constable.

"You don't pay any mind to that," Donald Houston answered.

"I'm writing down Daddy Means' name for constable on mine," Jeff Wheeler said.

"By God, so will I," Uncle George put in.

"What does a constable have to do?" the old man asked.

"Got to make arrests and take 'em in to the courthouse," Uncle George replied.

The men laughed at the thought of Daddy Means riding on his jenny for thirty-five miles to take a prisoner to jail. Gordon Hale came in then, with two men that were strangers to us, and there was a sudden silence, the kind that comes when someone we have been talking about enters a room.

Daddy Means was elected constable by a vote of five, but no one took it seriously except the old man himself, and he didn't know what to do about it.

"I wouldn't want to arrest a body unless he'd done me some harm," he said, shaking his head, bewildered.

In a one party state, the primary election is the only one of importance. The candidates went back to their homes, and we were forgotten for another two years.

The days continued hot and dry. We talked of nothing else when we met, now that the election was over, but the weather. Jock Wheeler could no longer boast of other drouths he had seen. This one, we knew, was the worst of all. As the time passed, adding to the weeks we had been without rain, we found ourselves boasting about it. Four weeks without rain. Five weeks. Six weeks, and seven. Never in all our years had we seen such a drouth as this one.

My garden, on the thin, sloping hilltop soil, suffered most of all. The moisture had long ago drained off or had been absorbed by the wild flowers we allowed to grow between the rows. When the hot wind blew over them, the withered plants swayed in a dance macabre, with their dry leaves rattling like dead men's bones. Bringing water to them had done no good, for the sun had baked them brown.

I gave up the thought of preserving any more food for the winter. There were a few jars of tomatoes and corn and beans, and of course there were the blackberries we had so persistently gathered and canned in the early summer. But there were still many shelves in the pantry with empty jars on them.

Even in the valley, where the land held its moisture longer, men were saying if the rain didn't come soon, all their crops would be ruined. A year's labor would be lost.

We heard the rain crow call, but nothing followed. Bob, and even Vannie, who did not like to kill, went out of their way to step on ants and spiders, to bring the rain, but it did no good.

A preacher came to the valley from the county beyond, to hold a meeting in the building where we had cast our vote and where the school was held. He came wearing overalls and he rode on the back of a mule. He asked for no money and no collection was taken up. In the spring and in the fall, he worked on his small farm, and when the crops were laid by in the summer, he went out to preach the gospel because he felt the call.

The people came from miles around to hear him. Wagons from the other side of the creek passed our place and strangers we had not seen before stopped by for a drink of water and to chat with us. We went down to the valley in one of the passing wagons, bouncing and jolting and falling against each other as we sat on the floor in the back. The houses we passed were empty, except the post office. Uncle George sat alone on his porch, with his chair leaning against the wall, stubbornly refusing to have anything to do with religion. I thought I saw a look of loneliness in his eyes as he watched us go by, the look a small boy has when he is left out of the play of other boys.

It was too early for the services when we arrived. The women walked through the graveyard, past the little mound where the Massery baby lay under a design of broken pottery, to a cedar grove behind the church, to hold a prayer meeting while we waited. Some knelt on the ground and others stood beside them in a circle. We joined Mag Massery and her mother-in-law who held little Ona astride her hip. Bob slipped quietly beside me and took my hand.

Lizzie Wells, silent even with her own kin, began to pray aloud. The evening was noisy with the sound of crickets and katydids, and the cry of the chuck-will's-widow. Now and then a child whimpered for its mother's breast, and the mules stamped impatiently at the hitching trees, creaking the wagons with each move. It seemed then that even the stars were moving in their course with clattering sounds. And through it all there came the soft voice of Lizzie Wells talking intimately with God.

The other women prayed, one after the other, Mrs. Wheeler, Mrs. Nixon and the Widow Johnson, and many

whom I did not know. There were no prayers to be mem-
orized and recited or read from a prayer-book. Each woman
spoke as if she were talking to an Intimate Friend, One
who stood in the circle with us and knew us well.

Darkness came and nothing could be seen but the light
cotton dresses of the women as they knelt and stood against
the black outline of the trees, and the shadowy forms of the
mules beside the wagons.

The lamps inside the church were lit and hung back on
the walls where they flared and sputtered and settled down
to a soft, steady flame. We went inside and took our places,
where the men were waiting, on the long school benches
with desks in front of us to rest our arms upon.

The preacher stood before us and spoke the words of the
Bible without the Book before him. It was said that he
could not read or write, but that he knew his *Bible* by heart
from cover to cover.

"And Elijah said unto Ahab, Get thee up, eat and drink;
for there is a sound of abundance of rain. So Ahab went up
to eat and to drink. And Elijah went up to the top of
Carmel, and he cast himself down upon the earth, and put
his face between his knees, and said to his servant, Go up,
now, look toward the sea. And he went up, and looked and
said, There is nothing. And he said, Go again seven times.
And it came to pass at the seventh time, that he said, Behold
there ariseth a little cloud out of the sea, like a man's hand.
And he said, Go up and say unto Ahab, Prepare thy chariot,
and get thee down, that the rain stop thee not. And it came
to pass in the meanwhile that the heaven was black with
clouds and wind, and there was a great rain."

He chanted the words and we were soothed by their sound

as well as their meaning. We stood for the hymn, when
the reading was over. The worried lines left the faces of the
men and women in the room, and our voices were full of
hope as we sang:

> Bringing in the sheaves,
> Bringing in the sheaves,
> We shall come rejoicing,
> Bringing in the sheaves.

I looked up to see Alan, who had come in quietly during
the reading, at our bench beside Vannie. Her eyes sparkled
happily as her voice blended with his in the song. Mag and
Jeff seemed not to notice the two together, but Granny
leaned over and whispered to me.

"It appears like Vannie's started a talking."

"She's rather young to start a talking," I said, using her
word for courting.

"I reckon," Granny answered, doubtfully. "Still and all,
there's no harm in talking. I was no more than her age
when I had my first baby."

Bill Wells was there, too, and his eyes searched often for
Vannie. He was handsome in the glow of the oil lamp above
his head. I wondered what the future held for him, with
his ambition to get on in the world. Would his life be more
of a success than his father's? Rufus, singing as he worked,
making things with his hands, did not look upon his life as
a failure.

The sermon was preached in the simple language of the
people. The preacher spoke of the prophets of old as if they
were no more remote than our own grandfathers, and we

felt that the God who came down to talk and walk with them in their time of need, could come down to us as well. Little Rock and Memphis were a world away, but Jerusalem was close to us then.

When the sermon was over, he called for the sinners to come up and be saved. But there were no sinners among us except a few young boys and girls who had grown to the age when they wanted to become church members. Two towheaded boys in clean overalls and a girl in a gingham dress went to the front to kneel before the mourners' bench.

There had been times when young rowdies and older men from Gordon Hale's place came to cut up in church, or to play practical jokes outside, by unhitching mules and driving them away, or taking wagon wheels from their axles. But they did not come that night. The drouth had affected us all, and even at Gordon Hale's they waited, hoping our prayers would bring rain to their corn.

The three children got up to say that they were saved, and we marched in a long line to shake them by the hand. There was a look of shy tenderness in the faces of their parents as they marched with us. The oil had burned low in the lamps and we knew by the moon that it was nearly midnight, when we finally turned toward our homes. There were the usual calls of "Better come spend the night with us."

Alan walked with Vannie and I could hear his voice behind me saying, "There's a piece of homestead land up on the slope near where you live. When I'm twenty-one I'm going to stake my claim."

"You won't go away to sing over the radio, then?" Vannie asked.

"No. I changed my mind about that."

They were like two voices, without bodies, one soft and tender, and the other boastful. The darkness had swallowed them completely. Two red eyes shone at us and they rose up in the air at our approach, like witches' eyes floating over us. We knew that it was a chuck-will's-widow flying off in fright.

"Is Uncle George a sinner?" asked Bob, who walked with me.

"No," I replied. "Why do you ask that?"

"Well, he wasn't there tonight, and he's always cussing."

Uncle George might curse a blue streak and give you the shirt off his back at the same time, while another would praise the Lord while he took it away from you. But I could not confuse Bob's mind with that now.

"Uncle George is not a sinner," I repeated.

The way up the hill was long and dark, and those who lived on the other side of Rocky Crossing spent the night in the valley. We stayed with the Masserys, and Alan stayed too. The Widow Johnson went home alone with her boys. I slept with Vannie and her grandmother, and I could hear the girl tossing restlessly beside me all during the night. The stars shone through the window, lighting the pallet on the floor where Alan lay with Bob, in all his clothes. At dawn he left us and went down to the home of his aunt, and Vannie's face was drawn from lack of sleep.

The sun shone down the next morning as mercilessly as ever, and those of us with little faith began to think we would never see rain again. We went back to Rocky Crossing to the same hard, baked earth. Grasshoppers, feasting on the withered plants, brushed against us and black crickets leaped before us in the grass. The days were still except for their cry. It seemed as though only we and the insects were left in a dying world, and they were waiting for us to go, to take over.

At last we saw a ring around the moon, and a cloud passed over the stars. A faint breeze stirred, bringing a damp smell, and the trees, still so long, were rustling their leaves like ladies in long silk dresses.

"Last night the moon had a golden ring, tonight no moon we see," I quoted.

"What does that mean?" Bob wanted to know.

"If we see a ring around the moon it means there's moisture in the sky and soon the rain clouds will come and cover it."

We sat on stones on the patio facing the rose garden, reluctant to leave the cool breeze that blew over us. Bob sighed happily.

"They never let me sit up late like this in Little Rock," he said. "Sometimes I even had to go to bed when it was still daylight and I didn't get to see the dark at all."

"Was that the reason you didn't like it there?" I asked, trying to be casual. Perhaps he was ready to trust me now.

"Well, I didn't have enough room to play, either. Just a little bitsy old yard with a fence around it, no bigger than this rose garden—not much bigger, anyway."

I told Bob then of the many boys in big cities who could only play in parks or on the streets, with nurses, even, sometimes to watch over the little ones. They had never seen the stars or the moon, I said.

"Gee, they must be mighty poor," Bob said.

"They are rich. We are the ones who are poor."

Bob laughed, for he thought I was joking.

All night the wind blew through the pines with the rustling sound of rain, and I got up many times to put out my hand, only to feel the dry breeze over it. Then, at the hour of dawn, when the furniture in the room and the trees outside changed from the black masses they had been, to take their true shapes in the grey light, I heard the sound of water falling on the roof and against the windowpane.

"Wake up, wake up," I called. "It's raining."

We took off our nightclothes and made our way in the dim light to the patio, to stand under the eaves and feel the rain fall on us. We passed a bar of soap from one to the other, and we were like ghosts seen dimly as we shouted and sang over the noise of the rain and turned around and around to feel the splash of cool water on all sides.

We put tubs and buckets out to catch the rain, and we went to our rooms and dressed. Morning came, bringing us a new-washed world. Every leaf and every blade of grass was bright and shining as if it had been scrubbed by careful hands. Still the rain fell. Lightning flashed and thunder growled and a tall pine standing near the house was struck. We could see the light zigzag down the trunk and leave its image printed where the bark was peeled. Then a pine behind the rose garden was struck. We were bombarded from all sides.

Jock Wheeler's stories came back to us of friends he had known that had been struck by lightning. The Widow Johnson's grandmother, he had heard tell, was sitting one day by the fire alone, nursing her baby and a-cussing God, when a bolt came down the chimney and struck her dead. The baby lived, he said. I had doubted the story, for I didn't know how the baby in her arms could escape the bolt that killed her. Besides, how did anyone know she was cussing God when she was sitting by the fire alone? But the lightning flashed again and we could see it strike the ground, and we were ready to believe anything.

"Lightning won't strike if you keep your feet in a pan of water," Vannie said.

There were other things to do in the storm besides sitting all day with our feet in a pan of water. I threw a towel over my head in a lull, and ran out to feed the chickens and turn the cow in the lot with the calf, then I came back to change my clothes for dry ones.

The yellow cat, called Snoopy, now, opened the screen door with her paw and came in out of the rain, proudly carrying a rabbit in her mouth.

"It's alive," Bob shouted, and he took it from the cat. "Look, it's alive. Let's kill it and eat it ourselves."

"No. Let's gentle it and keep it for a pet," Vannie said, stroking it between its ears.

Bob gave me the rabbit and I held it in my hands. The cat looked up, crying impatiently for the animal he had caught. He had planned to have a wonderful time with it, playing and teasing, pretending to let it go, only to catch it again, and finally eating it when it was too exhausted to play with any longer.

The little eyes stared at me in terror, and I could feel the heart beat against my palm. Four were pleading with me, one to cook it in a frying pan, one to keep it in a cage, one to torture it and eat it alive, and the little rabbit silently yearning for its freedom. I felt like Solomon, and it was the rabbit that won.

"Let's give it a sporting chance," I said. "I'll let it go. If it has learned its lesson, it will be safe and free. But if it hasn't and the cat catches it, he can have it. If you find it, Bob, we will eat it, and if Vannie finds it, we'll gentle it and keep it for a pet."

Vannie held the cat back while I opened the door and turned the rabbit out in the rain. A flash of lightning blinded us and we blinked our eyes, to find the rabbit gone when we opened them again. It disappeared from our sight, far away in the underbrush, hidden by a curtain of rain.

Chapter XIII

THE rain fell for three days, soaking deep in the earth. Then the sun shone and we saw the mountain, hidden so long behind the heat haze, stand out again, clear and purple. It seemed almost that the mountain moved. Sometimes, as now, it came so close that we wanted to reach out our hands and touch it. Then it ran away and hid out of sight on other days.

The birds came out once more to sing, and the chickens added their homely voices to the chorus as they pecked the soft earth for worms and bugs. The trees drank in the moisture and the fields in the valley turned green again. But the damage to our garden was done. Dry, dead leaves could not come back to life. A few new blossoms appeared on the withered plants, but they were like painted old women going on one last fling. Even the butterflies and the bees would have none of their pollen, and the fruit dried and fell off before it could grow. There were a few pumpkins and winter squash, and a little corn which we gathered and brought in to store, and nothing else.

We turned to the forest for our food. There were plums in the orchard of the old Lewis homeplace, and later the apples ripened. The presence of my ghost neighbor seemed to welcome us when we went to harvest her fruit in burlap bags. I liked to imagine her there in a faded cotton dress and a sunbonnet of the same material, with children clinging shyly to her skirts. When the first light frost came, the persimmons were sweet to eat, and no longer puckered our mouths. The wind blew down the hickory nuts and black walnuts, and we searched for them among the fallen leaves.

It was Bob who called these walks in the forest our treasure hunts. When the lessons were over and before time for the evening chores, we went off to search, not only for food, but for other treasures as well, rich pine knots for our winter fires, smooth flat stones to pave the patio and the garden walk, low-growing shrubs to plant in the border, or flowers to decorate our house; goldenrod, sunflowers, asters and the little evening primrose. Zozo went with us, and Snoopy, the cat, followed as far as he wanted, then he turned around and walked back home. Sometimes Adolphus waddled behind us, digging in the earth for treasures of her own.

The preparation for winter was all about us. When the sweetgum leaves began to fall, great, furry tarantulas came into our house seeking the warmth it would give them. We swept them out, only to have them with us the following day. The praying mantis that blended its green with the fresh spring leaves was now brown, like a brittle dead twig walking about. The squirrels buried nuts and acorns here and there, never trusting them all in one place, and the jays hid their food from other birds. Snakes we saw in our path were sluggish, moving slowly out of our way like sleepy children reluctant to go to bed.

Now the work season had come again to the valley. In the early dawn the men went out to their fields with their wives and children, even down to the least one, to gather their

crops, working until it was too dark to see. In the cotton
fields they walked slowly up and down the rows, dragging
long grey bags behind them, stopping at each plant to stuff
the white bolls in. In the corn and sorghum fields the green
stalks were cut and hauled off in wagons. And here and
there in the yards we saw a hog hanging to a limb of a tree,
scalded and scrubbed as pink as a newborn baby, waiting to
be cut in parts and smoked with hickory chips in a closed
room. An iron pot stood close by to render the lard.

Uncle George uncovered his sorghum mill and hitched
the two mules to tread the circle. It was fascinating to stand
there with the hickory and sweetgum leaves falling over us
and scattering their gold and red at our feet, while flocks of
warblers chattered overhead like nervous tourists afraid of
missing the next train. The mules turned patiently around,
with no show of curiosity as to why they were getting
nowhere with all their walking. The men brought the
sorghum they had harvested, and fed it to the mill, one
small bundle at a time, like fuel to a fire. And the sweet
juice came trickling out, dripping into a large barrel. Flies
and yellow jackets and bumblebees swarmed about, impatient to taste the sweet they could smell.

Bob stood close to Uncle George by the fire where the boil-
ing, bubbling juice dripped from one pan to another, turning darker and thicker in each successive pan. Uncle George
dipped off the skimmings with a large wooden spoon, and
Bob and the younger Wells boy and the Johnson boys caught
it with a stick. The skimmings from the last pan was like
molasses candy with a smoked hickory flavor. We took clean
sticks and dipped it up to eat our fill.

Uncle George kept a fourth of the syrup for his work

which he put up in gallon tins to sell. We bought two gallons for our winter supply, and we bought corn meal from Rufus Wells, who had made a grist mill from the motor of an old truck. Bill Wells, his oldest son, ground the grain that was brought each day in cotton bags. When it was done, he measured out an eighth which he kept back for his labor. His school at the county seat had begun, and he had much to make up, but he must wait until the harvest was over to go.

At Jock Wheeler's we dug sweet potatoes and he gave us half of all we gathered. Then the Widow Johnson, who had planted whippoorwill peas for her cash crop, sent word that she needed help to harvest them. We could work on equal shares, keeping half for our own needs.

Our work in the spring was solitary. We went out alone to plant the seeds and hoe the weeds away. And alone we watched the green plants grow, putting fertilizer on the soil when it needed it, pouring buckets of water as long as the well held out, and spraying and picking the insects away. But harvest time was a time of getting together. If Thanksgiving passed unnoticed in the mountains, it was because every day at harvest time is a day to give thanks. We felt close to God and close to each other then.

The Wells and the Wheelers and even the Masserys went down to help the Widow Johnson gather her whippoorwill peas. Mrs. Nixon and her two daughters worked, too, for part of the day. We saw them in the fields when we arrived, moving between the rows, picking peas and putting them in burlap bags. A patchwork quilt was spread on the ground for the babies to lie upon. Ona Massery, the little daughter of the Wells, and Virgil Johnson wandered here and there,

picking a few peas to put in their mothers' bags, then turning aside to play when they grew tired, chasing each other
up and down the rows with shouts of laughter.

"Perhaps you'd better help your own folks," I said to
Vannie when I saw how often her father stopped to take
out a plug of tobacco, or to talk to someone in the next row,
or stare at the sky, to see if it would rain. "Bob and I can
pick all the peas we'll need."

Vannie hesitated.

"I can pick enough for us both," she said. "I'll pick a spell
for them and I'll pick a spell for us."

Bob and I trailed behind her, for she was a faster picker
than either of us. Again I felt like Naomi watching Ruth as
she harvested in the field of Boaz, when I saw her bending
over a stalk to strip it with sure fingers, and move gracefully on to the next, dragging the bag behind her like the
train of a long skirt. Then Boaz appeared, wearing town
clothes, with his dark curly hair falling over laughing blue
eyes, and he walked beside her in the row. They picked
from the same plants and their hands often touched as they
pretended to be reaching for the same pod.

Bob stopped to play with a terrapin, poking it with a
stick to see it retreat into its shell. Then he found a grasshopper and put it in his pocket only to have it hop out,
spreading its yellow wings like a butterfly, beautiful in
flight, but ugly in repose. I picked on his side of the row as
well as my own, and Vannie and Alan went far ahead.

We met Rufus Wells and Bill on their way back, long
before we reached the end of our row. Vannie and Alan
moved on, without a glance in their direction, but I stopped
to talk with them.

"Now I'd call that a right nice mess for one meal," Rufus teased, looking down at my bag.

"My hands won't work as fast as yours," I replied.

We heard Jock Wheeler's voice a few rows beyond.

"I tell you it was a panther. No other animal would kill a full-grown deer and eat part and let the rest alone," he was saying.

"When did that happen?" I called out, as glad as Bob and Jeff Massery for the chance to rest.

"Just last night. Ben vows he saw a half-eaten deer off in the burnt woods where he was hunting. And I know none but a panther would do a thing like that."

"Didn't think there were any panthers around here," I said.

"Well, there's one now, I'm bound to say."

Rufus looked at me and smiled reassuringly. Then he went on his way and I went mine, down to the end of the long row, with Bob lagging behind. Our bags grew heavier with each step. I felt dwarfed by the long row before me when I turned around and started back. The plants bowed with the wind like waves coming toward me. We were like swimmers in a vast green sea, where some of us bobbed up and down in play and others swam steadily on.

The sun rose high, and beads of perspiration stood out on our foreheads. The wind was hot as it blew over us, pushing us impatiently along. Vannie stooped to pick a wild sunflower and put it in her hair. She looked as fresh and lovely as she did when we first came. Alan put a handful of peas in her bag and she playfully took them out and put them back in his.

"I won't be beholden," she said. "I'll pick my own myself."

There was a little scuffle, to give their hands a reason for meeting.

Mrs. Johnson had gone to the house earlier, and now she came out on the porch to blow the horn for dinner. It was a welcome sound to us. We left our bags where they stood and walked toward the kitchen. A hot fire still burned in the cook stove, and I sat on the porch steps while the men washed from the tin wash pan and went in to eat. Bob forgot now that he was tired and he played leap frog with the younger Wells boy and the Johnson boys. Vannie and Alan and Bill Wells and the Nixon girls chatted and laughed together, and Alan commenced to sing, with the others joining in.

The men ate quickly to make room for the women, and the young folks. Little heads peeped through the doors and windows and hungry eyes watched us when we sat down, but Mrs. Johnson had saved drumsticks of the fried chicken and peas and potatoes for them, and a pan of biscuits stood on the back of the stove keeping warm for them to butter and spread with peach preserves. We talked of the day's work. Some had picked one full bag and part of another, and some had picked even two. But my first one was scarcely more than half full, and Bob had far less.

The little children came rushing in when we left the table, and we started washing the dishes while they ate so that the Widow Johnson could get on soon with her picking. She had sat with the men only long enough to ask the blessing, as her husband would have done had he been alive. Then she said the same prayer with us, and now she took her place with the children and bowed her head again to pray.

When I returned to my row, I found a fuller, heavier bag waiting there than when I had left. I looked around at those in the rows near me, at Granny Massery and Mrs. Wheeler, but they were intent on what they were doing. Then I saw Rufus Wells bending over a stalk as if he did not know I was there. But there was a twinkle in his grey eyes which he could not hide.

The afternoon was long. The sun seemed to stand still in the sky. Bob grew restless.

"Looks like we've enough whippoorwill peas to eat the rest of our lives," he said.

"Looks like it to me, too," I agreed. "But let's don't give up till the others do."

He stumped his toe on a rock and he limped, dragging his heavy sack painfully behind him, to make my heart ache. The Johnson boys, younger than he, were working hard, and the younger Wells boy kept up with his older brother in the row. It would not be fair to them to see him standing idly by, or playing with the little ones.

"Where is Zozo?" I whispered to him. "I don't see her around. Go out and look for her."

Bob was off in a flash. Then he thought of his sore toe and stopped to limp. That held him back too much and he abandoned all thought of the toe to hurry on. The sun was sinking low when he returned with the dog trotting behind him.

"I had to look everywhere for her," he called out. "She was way down where the creek runs in the river. We'd lost her for certain sure if I hadn't gone to look for her."

Now he picked again with renewed energy, repeating, as he worked,

"You ought to see how glad she was when I came up. She'd never found her way back if I hadn't gone out to look for her."

Bob and I spent the night at the Nixons and Vannie went home with her people. The next morning we returned, to find Daddy Means there, picking, too. It was twilight before we started on our way up the hill, with a bag of whippoor-will peas on each back.

"You'd best stop at our house and spend the night," Rufus Wells said when he turned in his gate.

"Thanks, we must get on to our animals," I replied.

I saw from his expression that this was not the ordinary, polite invitation. Lizzie Wells, standing by, spoke up.

"Better tell them, Rufus," she said.

"Daddy Means said he saw something in the woods on his way here, like a big, yellow dog with a long tail, and it sprang up in a tree when it spied him. Now the old man is full of notions, I know, but he didn't hear about the half-eaten deer Ben Wheeler saw till he came down here. In reason there is a panther loose in the hills somewhere and you'd best not go up there after dark."

The cow had gone too long without being milked and the chickens and pig too long without being fed and watered. We had to go back.

"Then one of us will go with you," Bill Wells said when I refused.

"There's no need. You've plenty to do here. We'll hurry and get home before dark," I replied.

As we started on, Vannie, to cover my lack of etiquette, called back, "Better come go home with us."

We had the thrill of fear and possible danger on our walk

up the hill. The thick trees closed out the last rays of light. We could feel yellow eyes from behind every tree and rock in the darkness, and we heard soft, padded feet on all sides. Our footsteps on the soft dirt and fallen pine needles sounded thunderous. The harvest moon rose, blood red, and the shadows of the pines moved over the ground in the wind.

Late that night, after we had gone to bed, I was awakened by a scream.

"There's the panther," I thought, still half asleep.

The next morning I tried to remember the sound as I had heard it, but I could not bring it back to my mind. I spoke of it at the breakfast table.

"Likely as not it was a screech owl, or a hen calling out because she saw a snake in the dark," I said.

"It wasn't like a screech owl or a hen," Vannie put in. "It was a sound like I never heard before."

"You heard it too, then?" I asked.

"Yes."

Bob wanted to know how it sounded, and he felt a little cheated because he had not heard it, too.

We went often to the valley that autumn, bringing home food to be stored for the winter—peas, sorghum, corn meal, sweet potatoes.

"We ought to have a wagon to haul our things in," Bob said.

"When the first wheel was invented, that was the beginning of civilization," I said. "And we haven't even a wheel."

"We've got those wheels on the Ford. I could get me some lumber and make a wagon, and——"

I shook my head and he saw that was out.

"What did they make the first wheel out of?" Vannie wanted to know.

"I bet I know," Bob put in. "I bet they got a round log and cut a slice off and dug a hole in the middle for an axle. I'm going to make me a wagon with four slices of logs for wheels, and we'll use it to haul things in."

Our pantry was full of food. There was not as much as we had planned before the drouth, but it seemed to me to be an abundance, with the peas and sweet potatoes and pumpkins and row upon row of blackberries. Bob and I were like the Indians. We ate heartily. But Vannie looked anxiously at our stock.

"Reckon there's enough to see us through?" she asked.

"Surely there's enough there to last a lifetime," I laughed. She still looked unconvinced.

Wagons passed along the road loaded with cotton and sweet potatoes and corn to take in to market. Every day there were visitors who stopped to eat a meal with us, or to spend the night so they could get an early start the next morning.

There had been wood enough from the trees that were used to build our house to furnish us with firewood for many winters. It was Bob's job to gather it and pile it close to the house, and to draw water for the kitchen and wash-room. We soon found it as much a chore to remind him of it as to do the work ourselves. But he could work tirelessly on something he wanted to do. He sawed and hammered all day on some old lumber. His plans changed from a wagon to a two-wheel cart, and then to a wheelbarrow.

"Wheelbarrows are even better, 'cause you push them instead of pull them," he said.

It was finally finished, after a fashion, but the work of balancing it was greater than carrying the load, and Bob soon lost interest. The wooden wheelbarrow joined the Ford as another unused vehicle.

Next he made pine tar, working to the point of exhaustion rigging up a bucket to heat pine chips over a fire, with a stove pipe leading from a hole in the bucket to an old can. When the chips were hot, the melted juice ran through the pipe to the can in small trickles.

"That's real pine tar," he said after a hard day's work.

He was grimy and sweaty and his overalls were streaked with soot. But he was so proud and so tired that I hadn't the heart to tell him that there was nothing I needed less than pine tar just then. I put it on a shelf in the pantry instead, and drew a bucket of water myself for his bath.

There was a trunk in my bedroom filled with things I thought I would never need, and I wondered, in the beginning, why I ever brought it to the wilderness with me. There was a velvet evening wrap, evening dresses of the style worn then, and old coats with worn fur collars and frayed cuffs I had once loved and did not want to throw away. Now the trunk had become a kind of treasure chest where I could find anything I needed. I made a winter coat for Vannie from the evening wrap, and a jacket for Bob from an old suit of mine. And shirts and dresses were made from clothes long out of style.

The nights were colder now, and we built our first fire of the season. Vannie got down on her knees to light the pine kindling, and she watched it eagerly to see if it would burn. It flickered and died down, and she bent over to blow the flame until the wood caught. Then she leaned back to look on while it crackled and popped. If a fire goes out, your sweetheart does not love you, and if it burns—her eyes smiled as the flames leaped high up the chimney. There was a fluttering sound inside, and we thought of the chimney swallows who had nested there for the summer, now driven from their home.

Chapter XIV

DADDY MEANS came often to borrow a little salt or flour or sugar to be wrapped in an old newspaper, and the hour he chose was always the lesson hour. He came in quietly, so he would not disturb us and he took a chair outside our circle, pretending not to notice, but with ears intently listening.

"I dreamed and behold I saw a man clothed with rags, standing in a certain place with his face from his own house, a book in his hand, and a great burden upon his back," Vannie read from *Pilgrim's Progress*.

"That's like us coming from Uncle George's with packs on our backs," Bob said.

Our lessons were taken from the books we happened to have, from *A Little Boy Lost* and *Pilgrim's Progress*, Shakespeare and George Eliot and the *Bible*. And I searched in memory for things I had learned.

Vannie imitated my own speech when she first came to me, choosing the words I used, so that I had to watch myself closely, leaving out any slang or swearing that came to my mind.

"It ain't, I mean isn't," she said, or "I taken, I mean took," until at last she learned to say "it isn't" and "I took" quite easily. Then she went beyond me, and spoke in the language of the book we happened to be reading.

"Lo" and "verily" she often used. "I plucked some posies for that there, I mean that glass bowl," she said once. And again she came to me with "I found a place where serpents dwell out yonder by the chicken house."

When I saw she was ashamed of some of the words she had been using, words rich in meaning that I did not want her to lose, I began to use them, too. This puzzled her, and she was puzzled again when she read Juliet's words, "I am *afeard,* being in the night, all this is but a dream." She saw the word *tetchy* and many others she had once used and had come to believe wrong after she made her home with me, and she took them back into her vocabulary.

Vannie liked her reading lesson best, but Bob looked forward to geography. He didn't blink an eye when he learned that California was two thousand miles away. He still held to his story that he had been there and back in two days.

"What's on the other side?" he asked.

"The Pacific Ocean," I replied.

"Then what?"

"Islands. Lots of islands, then Australia, Japan, China."

"Tell about them."

"Later. We haven't finished with Europe yet."

We drew large maps from a small one in the dictionary, and I tried to make these countries more than colored places on a sheet of paper, with creeping lines for rivers and shady places for mountains and small dots for cities. I told of places I had visited, of people I had seen in English villages, of children playing in the Paris streets and the songs that were sung in Italy.

Far away from human kind as we were, we were lonesome, in our solitude, for all the people in the world. They were human beings, as we were, with two feet that walked the earth, two hands that did the work upon it, two eyes that saw the same beauty we saw, clouds and hills and stars, and a mouth to say the same things, in their own way, that we said.

When I told of a Russian I had known, homesick for the cold, snowy plains of his country, and a German, who planted in his California garden all the flowers he had loved in his old home, Vannie and Bob looked upon them as their friends, too, and wanted to know more about them.

"Did you ever know a Chinaman?" Bob asked.

"Yes. I knew a Chinaman, a very learned man, and I knew a Japanese girl in Honolulu who wore a kimono with a pretty colored sash which she called an *obi.*"

"Tell about them."

"One thing at a time, Bob," I protested.

Sometimes, when my father sent magazines, he included a few newspapers. Several days passed before they reached me, and the news of the bonus army in Washington, or the winter styles without corsets designed by Patou, were old to us then. But the things we read from the old books were new, the servant of Elijah looking hopefully toward the heavens for a rain cloud, and Ruth harvesting in the field of Boaz.

Once I threw some old newspapers in the fire when Daddy Means was there. He grabbed them quickly before they had time to burn.

"Don't never throw such things away," he said.

"Do you want them?"

"Yes. I'll take them if you don't want them."

I did not remind him that he could not read.

"If there are any books you want to borrow, you're welcome to them," I went on.

He hesitated.

"I'd be beholden for one or two of those yellow and red books," he said.

I gave him the copies of *Atlantic Monthly* and *Harpers* that he indicated. Later, when he returned them, carefully wrapped in a flour sack to keep clean, he told me everything that was in them. Wouldn't Uncle George be surprised, I thought. I could hardly wait to tell him.

"Is there anything else you'd like to borrow?" I asked.

Daddy Means looked over the books on the shelves.

"This looks like it might be a good one," he said, pointing to Thoreau's *Walden*.

"*Walden* by Henry David Thoreau," he said. "That's a good book."

He pronounced the name as it should be pronounced. Only an educated man would know that. Who was Daddy Means and what was his life before he came here? I wondered. What could have been his reason for pretending all these years he could not read or write?

I decided then that his secret was his own. I would keep it for him. And when I saw Uncle George patiently explaining to him again where to put his mark for his signature, I said nothing, though the temptation was great.

The days were crisp and cool, and night came early. The crickets and the katydids were silent and the birds that stayed on, flew noiselessly about, with no more than chirping sounds. There were other noises in the forest now, the

sound of wild geese crying in their flight to the south, sometimes the howl of a wolf and now and then the short, yelp-
ing bark of a fox that passed by. And there were sounds we
must listen close to hear above the whisper of the pines and
the running creek, the sound of sweetgum balls and walnuts
falling on the ground and the seed pods rattling in the redbud trees. And when the wind blew hard, the softer noises
were covered by a loud moan, with branches scraping
against the windowpanes and walls like bony fingers scratch-
ing to be let in.

The hunters' moon rose full and red. It slowly climbed
until it shone through my bedroom window, waking me
from a sound sleep. The long slant of light on my pillow
was like a finger beckoning me outdoors to a world that was
different from the daytime world. I could see the tree tops
through my window take on strange shapes. Sometimes they
were boats at sea, sailing in the wind, sometimes old crones,
scolding and nodding their heads in anger at each other,
and sometimes they were giant children playing a game of
tag, reaching out to touch one another without running
away. Bells tinkled as a herd of mules or cows grazed in
the dark, moving closer, then wandering away again. And
far off in the distance, I could hear dogs barking, with
shrill, excited barks and deep, clear ones, like a chorus of
bass and soprano voices. Some animal of the forest was
crouching high in a tree or hiding under a mound of earth,
ready to fight for its life.

I got out of bed and threw a coat over my nightgown,
and put on some shoes. I could hear Vannie restlessly tossing
in her bed as I tiptoed through the living room. It was late,
I knew, for the fire had burned out, and the ashes looked

cold in the moonlight. There were sweet potatoes in the hollow of the wagon thimbles that served as andirons, and on the hearth there was an iron skillet with a squirrel stewing and a pot of whippoorwill peas.

"Can't you sleep, Vannie?" I asked.

"No, the moon's keeping me awake," she replied.

"Then draw your curtains."

"I don't want to. I like to see it."

We laughed softly so we would not awaken Bob, asleep on his cot in the kitchen.

"So do I," I replied. "I'm going out for a little walk. Want to come along?"

In a twinkling Vannie had on her coat and shoes, and we went quietly out the front door. Zozo heard us and she left her bed under the house, and the cat appeared suddenly before us, to follow, too.

"Where are you going?" Bob called before we reached the gate.

"For a little walk," I answered.

"I want to go, too! Wait for me!" he started out as he was.

"Go back for your coat. It's chilly."

"I'm not cold. Will you wait for me if I go?"

"Yes. I promise."

The black beady eyes of birds and little furry creatures that must have stared at us from the forest, saw a strange procession that night by the light of the moon as we walked along the road, with light nightgowns and pajamas showing beneath the dark coats, followed by a dog and a cat. Our moving shadows seemed more solid than we who made them, for they showed black and firm against the silver ground. Far away I saw a red glow in the sky like the light of dawn, but it faded and was gone as we walked on, instead of growing lighter. Perhaps it was what they called the false dawn, I thought.

Leaves blowing from the trees flew before us like the shadows of birds. I wondered what I would choose to look at last if I were given only one minute more to see with my eyes. I thought of dewdrops on a spiderweb, sparkling in the sun, wild geese flying overhead, hills in the distance catching the last red rays of the sun. I decided then that it was moonlight in a pine forest, with a small, clear creek to catch it on its ripples, that I would want to keep with me after my eyes are gone.

The dogs continued their baying and I knew that the animal, crouching somewhere in the shadows, was still alive. Cowbells sounded above the singing of the water and we heard the steps of the mules and the sorrel mare pass close to us. Sounds were clearer because of the night. And we smelled crushed leaves and the damp earth on the banks of the creek, which we could not smell during the day.

We stepped over the stones of the creek to cross to the other side. Here the cat turned back, for he had had enough of night prowling.

A snake crossed the road ahead of us, and we stood where we were to let it pass. It was followed by another, and another and another, creeping like long, dark shadows before our eyes. They were migrating to their winter den, where they would lie close together in a writhing mass until spring, when the earth turned warm again. I do not know how long it was, nor how many passed. We stood as if we were hypnotized, moving our eyes to and fro in fascination as we saw them appear, one after the other, and lose themselves in the

shadows. We did not move. We scarcely breathed. It was
as though we were looking on at the creation of all the
snakes in the world. Even the dog sat close beside us and
made no sound.

There was no feeling of repulsion as I have had when I
came upon one snake alone in my path, but we stood there
in awe, even after the last one had gone. Then we turned
around and walked home in silence.

We could not go back to bed and sleep after that, so we
built up the fire. A cricket, hidden between the stones, felt
its warmth and began to sing. The peas in the pot started to
bubble and boil and steam rose from the skillet with the
stewed squirrel in it. We knew then we were hungry and
we brought plates from the kitchen and pulled our chairs
up close to the fire to eat the whippoorwill peas and squirrel
and baked sweet potatoes. The moon went down, and the
fire gave the only light. Then the darkness of the windows
turned slowly to the grey of dawn. We went back to bed
at the hour when those in the valley were getting up to
begin their day.

Daddy Means did not come that day at the lesson hour.
But later, as we sat down to supper, he drove up in his
wagon, coming from the direction of the valley. When he
walked in, we invited him to sit at the table with us.

"I passed here this morning and I called loud enough to
wake the dead, but nobody answered," he said. "In reason,
I thought, there was nobody home."

"We were here," I replied. "We overslept this morning."

I didn't say we had been awake half the night, with a
walk in the moonlight and a supper at dawn. Even to

Daddy Means, who was called "tetched" and queer-turned, this would sound too crazy.

"Well, you sure slept sound," he said. "My house burned down last night."

"How! When!" we wanted to know.

"Don't know how nor when. I was out possum hunting with my dogs last night and I came home to find it smouldering in ashes."

The reddish glow I saw in the east that I thought was the false dawn was from the flames of the old man's house.

"It didn't get my clothes because the night was cold and I had them all on," he went on. "But it just about got everything else in the place."

Vannie looked at me and there was a message in her eyes which I could not read. I was sorry for the old man, but after all, his loss was small. The little log hut could be rebuilt from logs in less than a week, and the furniture he had made of rough lumber could be made again.

"You'd better stay here, then," I said. "We'll fix a pallet in the room here with Bob."

I was not enthused over having him make this his home, though I could not do otherwise. But Daddy Means liked his privacy, too.

"I still got the potato house. The fire didn't come that far. But I got nothing else."

Vannie had the same look of humiliation that she sometimes had when I sat down to the table with my company instead of standing beside them to serve them. Daddy Means was embarrassed. Then he spoke again.

"Been down in the valley to tell them about my fire.

Uncle George gave me two new pairs of overalls, the Widow Johnson gave me some jars of corn and tomatoes she'd put up, Lizzie Wells gave me a couple of quilts, and——"

I took the hint at last. I thought of the things I owned, and I brought out some dish cloths and towels, and I gave him an iron skillet, a stewing pan and a plate and cup and saucer. A look of relief came over Vannie's face.

"It sure makes a fellow feel good to know he's got friends when a thing like this happens," the old man said.

He took the things I gave him to the wagon and drove off. We lit the lamps and built up the fire, and again our cricket began to sing. Bob searched until he found it, hidden in the crack of the floor.

"Let's keep it in a jar with some dirt and grass so it will stay alive and sing all winter," Vannie said.

But the cricket, imprisoned in the jar, sang no more.

Chapter XV

IN THE wilderness, where there were no living beings around us, except the animals in the barnyard and the wild creatures we seldom saw, when each day was like another in the chores that must be done, we knew instinctively when Sunday came. Even with a calendar, we often forgot the days in the rest of the week, and had to count back to some event in the past to know whether it was Wednesday or Thursday. Perhaps there was something in the atmosphere that came up from the valley, when men put on their clean overalls and rested on the Sabbath from their work in the fields, and women, in their best dresses, cooked a big dinner and visited among themselves. We would have known that day without a calendar.

So it was with Christmas. We could feel it in the air, even without the gaily lighted shops of town and the Salvation Army Santa Clauses ringing bells before their iron pots. The days were short. We lit the lamps early and we got up while the moon was yet in the sky. But the sun was still warm. It might have been early autumn or late spring. The brown leaves clung stubbornly to the oaks, and now and then in the forest we could see the last red and yellow of the sweetgum and hickory. The only sign of winter was in the holly trees and the red haws by the creek, with their bright red berries, and the black locusts, showing thorns that had been covered with leaves all summer, like cats' claws stretching out from padded feet.

Bob remembered a Christmas tree at the orphanage, with a dressed-up Santa Claus and gifts for all the children, but Christmas to Vannie had been like any other day except there were firecrackers and perhaps a stick of peppermint candy and store-bought cheese from Uncle George.

We baked a raisin cake and plum pudding and we put a hen in a coop to fatten her for the feast. And we made presents to give to one another. Because Bob had come to expect it and Vannie had never had it, we must have the best Christmas celebration ever.

I looked again at my trunk, filled with things I once thought I could never use here, and found an old sweater which I ripped apart to knit into scarfs for Vannie and Bob, with wooden needles Rufus Wells had made for me. Bob borrowed my sharp paring knife to whittle wooden spoons for us, and Vannie made a patchwork sofa pillow for me and a bandana handkerchief for Bob out of scraps of gingham. She made a handkerchief for Alan, too, but it was white, from a linen pillow case that was beginning to wear, and she embroidered a dainty *A* in the corner. We tried at first to hide our gifts from each other, but we soon gave that up as hopeless and worked boldly on them by the light of the lamp in the evening.

Jeff Massery came by in his wagon on the week before Christmas with his family, and they spent the night with us.

"They're giving away flour at the county seat," he said. "The Red Cross is giving away flour and maybe other things to anybody suffering from the drouth. Want me to bring you some, too?"

Jeff's crops had suffered as much by his neglect when he left his farm to work on the road as by the drouth. It was a ride of two days each way in the wagon, and the energy spent in going and coming would have bought several sacks of flour. But Jeff Massery could not resist getting something for nothing.

We spread pallets on the floor, and Granny Massery slept on the sofa in the living room. The stars were still shining the next morning when Jeff went out to hitch the mule to the wagon, to start on their way.

"I'm not in the notion to go," Granny Massery said. "I aim to stay on here where I am."

She stood at the door with me as we saw them go off in the dim half-light. When they were out of sight, she turned to me and said, "Somehow it goes against me to be a-begging for my bread."

She was like a little bird flitting about the house, with her long, full skirt swishing as she walked, and her bright eyes taking everything in. She did as much work as the rest of us put together, without seeming rushed about it.

Bob had a wart on his hand and she took it off with magic. Every day at a certain hour by the sun, she put tobacco juice on it, from the snuff she used, and mumbled words so softly no one could hear. She would not tell me what they were, though I begged her to do so.

"Nobody knows but me," she said, "and when I die the secret goes with me."

Eventually the wart disappeared and she looked upon it as proof of her secret power.

She knew of many cures; of teas and broths to mix and brew for healing the sick, of how much clay a woman must eat when she's reached the period of crossing over, and she knew which phases of the moon and stars made the cures more potent. Some of this knowledge she had passed on to Vannie, and then to me, but some she kept secret.

She talked about the valley in the old days, when she was a young girl, and sang old ballads that she used to sing. Vannie had been ashamed of them because they were old-timey, but I listened to her high, quavering voice singing, "Where have you been, O Arnold, my son," and *Barbary Allen*.

A sparkle came into her eyes when she remembered the dances and play parties and the young men waiting at the church door to take her home from meeting.

"I wasn't without sparkers to come a-talking with me," she said.

I remembered the stories about Granny's youth, how it was told even that Jeff was not old Massery's son, but no one could say for sure. All that was known was that he was born too soon after the wedding.

"I've lived a long time," the old woman went on, "and there's little of life that I've missed. Still and all, I can't say there's a thing I've ever done I'm sorry for."

When the Massery wagon came back, four days later, with their Red Cross flour, Granny still refused to go with them.

"I'll stay on a spell longer," she announced.

She entered into the spirit of Christmas preparations, going down to the creek with us to gather holly and cedar and red haw berries, and she gave Bob a boost up the sycamore tree to gather the mistletoe that clung to the high branches. We put some in vases, and made wreaths with the rest, and we decorated the whole house, even to the washroom window. A pine sapling mounted on a wooden block was our Christmas tree. It stood in the center of the long living room, looking festive with its gay strings of red haw berries and fluffs of white cotton and little gingerbread men and cookie stars and crescents hanging on its branches.

We had made rag dolls for Ona and the little Wells girl, with black eyes and long eyebrows painted in ink, and a cupid's-bow mouth with lipstick red. Bob cut off some of the well rope and untwined it for the hair, which was blond and curly, sewed on their stuffed heads. Granny made their dresses from scraps, with wide, full skirts flaring out to show their white drawers and petticoats.

On Christmas Eve we went down to the valley, but Granny still would not go home. She stayed to look after the house for us. We left a doll for Lizzie to give her daughter on Christmas morning, and some gingerbread cookies for the boy. Then we took the other doll to Ona. The child grabbed it in delight, and rocked it in her arms, crooning to it as her Granny crooned to her. Then she brought out the stick whittled in the shape of a doll and rocked them both, to show no partiality. She put them together on a rag spread on the floor for a pallet, to sleep side by side.

At Uncle George's store we bought oranges and apples and nuts which he had in stock once a year, and some firecrackers and shells for the rifle, for Christmas is not Christmas in the backwoods without guns shooting and crackers popping. Donald Houston, from beyond the valley, drove up in his wagon with a beef he had killed. For twenty-five cents I bought the choicest cut. Filet mignon for Christmas dinner! We would have a feast. The hen could come out of her coop, free to lay eggs again.

With our burlap bags stuffed with supplies and packages that had come for us through the mail, we went back home. Granny had a bright fire burning, and supper waiting on the table.

"Somebody came by and left this for you," she said, bringing out a quart jar of white corn whiskey.

Now and then someone in the valley rigged up a homemade still in the forest and made a little corn whiskey for himself and his neighbors. There was not the secrecy that there was about Gordon Hale's place, for it was not made to be bought and sold stealthily. It was not an unusual gift to be left at our house from one who passed by on his way home from his hidden still.

"Want a hot toddy?" Granny asked.

I shook my head. I was too tired after the long hike to drink fresh, raw whiskey.

"Let's keep it for Christmas eggnog," I said.

The Christmas parcels were put under the tree and the gaily colored greeting cards we received were hung on the branches with strings.

Granny came in my room the next morning at dawn, to waken me, with a glass in each hand.

"I fixed you a hot toddy," she said, giving me one of the glasses and keeping the other for herself.

It was strong, and I was wide awake after one sip.

"We always had hot toddy in the morning before breakfast when I was a young one," she went on, sitting on the bed to watch me while I dressed. "Pa never sat down at the table without drinking his toddy first."

Vannie and Bob squatted on the floor beside the tree to open the Christmas parcels. We pretended surprise at the ones we gave each other, but their hands pulled eagerly at strings and red ribbons on the gifts from my relatives and friends. They tore at Santa Claus labels and Red Cross seals and pushed aside mountains of tissue paper, to see the real surprises waiting for them, warm sweaters and stockings, and two boxes of chocolate candy.

The toddy Granny had mixed made me feel gay.

"But eggnog is what we want for Christmas morning," I said.

I went to the kitchen to beat two eggs separately, with two tablespoons of sugar, and added a quart of rich milk. Then I poured in the whiskey by guess, tasting it often to see when I had enough. Granny drank a glass with me, but she shook her head.

"Nothing beats a toddy, hot or cold, as a fellow says," she remarked, and she mixed another one for us in her way. "Now you see if you don't like this better."

"Let me taste! Let me taste!" Bob exclaimed.

Granny looked at me inquiringly, but I shook my head.

"Run along now, with your presents, till we get breakfast," she said.

But she was still unconvinced.

"Still and all," she added in a lowered voice to me, "when I was a young one, we kept a bottle on the table and Pa used to pass it around, even to the least one."

I had heard my father say the same thing, and it had not hurt him, nor had it made him a drunkard. He grew up

strong and was never sick a day, and I can not remember
seeing him drink at all until the prohibition law was passed.
I think he did then, only in protest rather than from desire.
Still I shook my head stubbornly.

The room was beginning to spin around and around very
slowly and the floor surged as I walked. Vannie and Bob
were eating apples and oranges and nuts, and I thought of
my own childhood, when the fruit in the stocking hanging
from the mantel was much more tempting than food on the
breakfast table.

I saw my reflection in the mirror staring back at me. And
I wondered if all my life was behind me at thirty-three. Or
was there a future ahead to look forward to. What was it
and where would I find it? I wondered.

"Want me to fry the meat for breakfast?" Granny asked.

"No," I replied quickly. "I'll broil that steak myself over
hot ashes, and we won't have it for breakfast."

I had eaten possum and sweet potatoes and gingerbread at
Jock Wheeler's for breakfast, and I had eaten roast squirrel
and whippoorwill peas and sweet potatoes before dawn when
we had seen the migration of snakes. We did not live by
clocks, it was true, but I was going to have my Christmas a
traditional one.

"I want some of the raisin cake now," Bob said.

"You'll have nothing now but eggs and bread and milk,"
I replied.

Vannie brought out the tablecloth to set the table and I
stopped her.

"We'll have breakfast in the breakfast nook in the kitchen
and we'll wait and eat our Christmas dinner here at noon."

"Still and all," Granny said, "the sun is climbing high and it's so late we'll not want to eat at noon if we have breakfast now."

I was stubborn.

"Then we'll wait till the sun comes in a straight line when we open the south door before we eat at all."

Granny milked the cow, Vannie went out to feed the chickens and pig, Bob brought in the wood and drew two buckets of water from the well, and I made the beds and tidied the house. I saw Granny take a drink of whiskey from the jar without a chaser, after she had skimmed the milk, and I envied her. I tried to do the same, but it was like fire in my throat and I had to drink eggnog to take the burning taste away.

The sun slant moved slowly over the living-room floor until it was a straight line in the center. We brought in the table and put the prettiest cloth on it, with a bowl of holly leaves and red haw berries in the center. I held the steak over the coals in a long-handled toaster, and the heat from the fire made me feel giddy. There came over me a feeling of well-being.

The floor rolled before me as I walked to the table to put the steak on the platter. I tried to be dignified and serious, and I heard the children giggle. How could Granny do it? I wondered. She had taken twice as much raw corn whiskey as I, but it had no more effect on her than so much water.

The steak was tender and juicy. It was the first meat I had had in a year except chicken and squirrel and rabbit, with now and then some possum or a slice of venison some hunter passing that way would leave.

"Didn't know that old cow of Donald Houston's could taste so good," Granny said, reaching for a second helping.

It wasn't pleasant to be reminded of the personality of the animal I was eating, but I said nothing. I forced myself to take another bite, for it was delicious.

"Poor man, never did seem to have any luck with his cattle," Granny went on. "Same thing happens to them all, it seems."

"What happens to them?" I asked.

"Oh, it don't hurt the meat a bit. It's just that they can't find their calves."

"Abortions?"

This was a word one must not use before children, and Granny was embarrassed. She nodded her head, and glanced to see if they had heard.

"But it don't hurt the meat a bit," she repeated.

I pushed my plate aside, and the cat and dog had tender steak for their Christmas dinner that day.

"Granny," I said, turning the conversation so the plum pudding would not be spoiled for me, too, "who brought the whiskey?"

"That Alan boy," Granny replied.

I was sorry I had asked that question. Vannie looked up quickly, her eyes like a startled fawn's.

"Did he say anything?" she asked, shyly.

"No. Just that he's decided to work a spell on the Gordon Hale place and he brought us this for our Christmas toddy."

"Look, Vannie," I said, drawing her attention to me, "this is the way to light the plum pudding."

I heated the rest of the whiskey in the jar to pour over the pudding, and I quickly lit it. It went up in a blue flame and died down again. Vannie was quiet while we finished the dinner, and I tried to bring back the gaiety I had felt earlier.

"Granny," I said, "let's have a dance. We'll have it while you are here with us."

"You've a good house for one," she replied.

The young people of the valley had wanted me to give a dance for some time. The living room and dining room were large and could open into one long room when the monk's cloth curtains were drawn back. And there were no beds to take apart and move out of the way, except Vannie's couch. We made our plans and Vannie could not resist joining in, as any girl of fifteen would do.

"Jeff's father was such a dancer as I've never seen," Granny mused. "Up to the day he died, he could cut a shine that put the young folks to shame."

"Do you mean Mr. Massery?" I asked in surprise, for I had heard of his wooden leg.

"Of course. I said Jeff's father," Granny replied.

I was properly chastised, and I asked no more. We got up to wash the dishes and I saw Vannie pick up the empty fruit jar Alan had brought the whiskey in and take it to her room. At fifteen, even an empty fruit jar can be a romantic thing.

"First love is one you never forget," I said as my eyes followed the girl.

"First love and last love. They are the only ones that count. And last love is the best of all," Granny said.

"How does one know last love?" I asked.

"You know it, all right. There's no mistaking last love."

I could see my past and my future in Vannie and her

grandmother. I had found romance in things as foolish as empty fruit jars. But when I grow old, though I might say with Granny that there's little in life I've missed, I think I can add, as she did, "Still and all, I can't say I'm sorry for a thing I've ever done."

Chapter XVI

BEN WHEELER passed our house with his dogs and gun to hunt squirrels, and we told him of our plan to give a dance. The news spread far and wide. Our guests started coming at sundown on the day we had named, and they kept coming until late in the night. They came in wagons, on horseback and afoot over many miles. Young girls in freshly washed cotton dresses, with their hair crimped and curled, and boys in clean overalls, with shoes on their feet, and old folks bringing their children with them. There were some whose names I did not know and whom I had never seen before, and when they left, I was not to see them again, for they lived in settlements far beyond the valley.

The Wheelers were the first to arrive, for it was Ben who started the grapevine system on its way, and the Masserys came soon after. We had not had our supper, so we added more peas to the pot and made up more cornbread, and asked them to sit with us. When we were through, we moved the furniture from the living room and Vannie's room into the kitchen, and we placed the chairs against the walls to clear the floor for the dance. Jock Wheeler made benches of rough lumber, left from the building, resting on upturned log stumps. Here the married women sat, holding their children in their laps as they watched the young folks frolic.

Jim Carter and his daughter came with their fiddles to play for us. I had not known them before, but Ben had sent word especially for them to come. They were religious people and looked upon dancing to fiddle music as a sin. But they loved nothing better than playing and they never missed a chance to go where music was wanted, fiddling tirelessly while others danced in sin. They laughed with us at their inconsistency.

The fiddles were tuned and the music commenced. They played *Eighth of January*. The girls, sitting with the older women on the benches, looked up expectantly, but the boys leaned against the wall, each waiting for the other to make the first move. The music played on to the end. Then there was more tuning of the strings, and the fiddles began to play *Arkansas Traveler*.

"Come on," Ben Wheeler whispered to me. "Let's you and me start."

Three other couples came up and we joined hands, circling to the right and to the left, dancing to the call of old Jock Wheeler. Vannie danced with us, but her eyes looked often through the window into the darkness, searching for someone who had not come. Each time the door opened, she turned eagerly toward it, and I found myself watching, too, as the late guests arrived. Rufus and Lizzie Wells entered, with their small children, when I was beginning to wonder if they had not been told about the dance at all. I wished their son Bill could have been with them too, to dance with Vannie.

At last Alan arrived, walking under the mistletoe that

hung above the door, and with him was the young daughter of Donald Houston. She was about Vannie's age, but she was buxom, with bold eyes that flirted as she looked about the room. Vannie had the expression of one who had been slapped. It lasted only an instant, and she went on with the dance as if she had not seen them. If I had not known her, I would have thought she was having the time of her life, then. Her eyes no longer searched through the darkness of the windowpane. She went gaily from one partner to another, sashaying and promenading in the square dance. Alan watched her with puzzled eyes, but she gave no sign that she knew he was there.

My house was never so lovely to me as it was that night. A soft light shone from the oil lamps and the two blazing fires on the ceilings with their hand-hewn crossbeams and rafters, bringing out the rich, warm color of the pine. It brightened the women's dresses and the men's overalls as they surged in and out of the rooms. There was a smell of the earth in the room that night, and of men and women who live close to it. I felt a part of them, then.

The music stopped and I could hear the talk of the men who had gathered in the kitchen to drink corn whiskey, passed around from one to another in a quart fruit jar.

"That time I traded my shotgun to Daddy Means," began Jock Wheeler, who had gone out to join them. "Slipped up one day when he wasn't home and drove nail holes in the trunk of that big old hickory tree beside the pond. Then I went again with my gun that wouldn't shoot shucks. 'Try it out on yonder hickory, Daddy Means,' I said. Well, he took it and shot it, and when he saw all the holes in the tree, he said, 'By gum, a gun that'll shoot that far is something to have!' He like to a-traded all the tobacco he had for that there gun."

There was loud laughter. The women, in the front rooms pretending not to listen, smiled too.

"I wasn't fooled. I could see those were nail holes in that tree," Daddy Means spoke up.

Rufus Wells came up to me when the fiddles played again. His large hand, rough from hard work, closed over mine as we joined in the dance. Now Alan had chosen Vannie for a partner. Eight of us danced around in a circle one way and then the other. Then Rufus held my hand alone.

> Pass your partner and take the next.
> Ladies swing in and gents swing out.

Jock Wheeler's call, in his singsong voice separated us, but our eyes searched and found each other, then we were together again.

> Left Allemande with your left hand
> Right to your partner——

His hand closed firmly over mine, then he let it go again, and another hand came to take its place.

> Swing that pal and swing that girl,
> Swing your partner round in a whirl!

Rufus Wells put his arms around my waist to whirl me around, and his cheek touched my hair as he bent down to whisper, "Somebody's looking mighty sweet tonight."

He held me close, then let me go for someone else to swing. As I turned around I saw Lizzie Wells under the wall lamp with the baby in her lap and the little girl leaning against her arm asleep. There was an expression of such beauty on her face as she bent down over the little one, with the light shining on her hair, that I felt a pain almost physical. Things seen in the light of an oil lamp, standing in relief against the darkness of a room, stay in the memory long after other scenes are forgotten. She was the eternal mother, the Madonna of Bethlehem, of Florence and Flanders and of the hills of Arkansas.

> Ladies to their seats and gents all follow,
> Thank the fiddler and kiss the caller.

The dance was over. I left Rufus and went to his wife.

"Lizzie," I said, "why don't you dance the next set with Rufus?"

Lizzie smiled, a little embarrassed, and said, "I'd be a sight prancing up there. I've not danced since I was knee high."

"I've never danced this way before," I went on. "It'll come back to you the way it came to me."

"But the young one. He won't go to sleep."

"I'll take him, then," I said, holding out my arms for the child.

Granny Massery, whose keen black eyes missed nothing, and who, I am sure, knew all my inmost thoughts, took up the little girl and gently carried her into the bedroom where there were children and a few old folks stretched out across the beds and on pallets spread on the floor. I followed with the baby and Lizzie got up to go to her husband, turning to look back, with an embarrassed laugh, to the women on the benches.

"There's something gets hold of a body when the fiddles play and your feet are a-stepping," Granny said.

She put the little Wells girl on the bed where other children lay sound asleep, and she tiptoed out of the room for fear of missing something. I sat by the window, rocking the child in my arms and singing to him softly so the others would not awaken.

> A frog went a-courting and he did ride,
> M hmmm, M hmmm,
> A frog went a-courting and he did ride
> With a sword and a pistol by his side,
> M hmmm, M hmmm.

From where I sat I could see the dancers as they moved to and fro past the door. The sound of their feet pattering to the fiddle music kept time to my song. Rufus' eyes turned toward my room, but he could not see me in the dark. Quiet little Lizzie was flushed and pretty as she sashayed in and out, dancing away from him and going back again. The Houston girl danced too, flirting with all who swung her around, but Alan and Vannie were not within my vision. Bob left the Johnson boys he had been romping with and came in the room to me.

"I'm sleepy," he said.

The baby stirred when he spoke and he lowered his voice.

"I've no place to go. Everywhere I look there's somebody asleep."

Through the closed window we could hear the sound of

mules and horses tied to trees across the road, stamping and pawing the ground, and now and then the voices of men as they went out to drink the whiskey they brought with them. There were footsteps that came close and paused.

"There's Vannie with Alan," Bob said in an excited whisper. "Look! He's kissing her. I'm going to tease her tomorrow."

The sound of Alan's voice came but I could not hear the words. Then Vannie answered, tenderly, "I can't, Alan. Not now, I can't."

"Bob," I said, drawing him away from the window, "get one of those quilts in the linen closet and spread it down here to sleep on."

He made his pallet at my feet and lay down to sleep in all his clothes. I started to put the baby down too, but he woke up with a cry and I rocked him faster and sang a little faster too, as if that would put him quickly to sleep.

He took Miss Mousie on his knee,
M hmmm, M hmmm.
He took Miss Mousie on his knee,
Say, Miss Mousie, will you marry me?
M hmmm, M hmmm.
Say, Miss Mousie, will you marry me?

Should I raise the window and call Vannie in, I wondered. Alan's voice was cool now as he spoke.

"We'd best go on in and dance, then."

"Some other time I can come to you. Let me come some other time," Vannie spoke with none of her little girl shyness now.

"All right, if you want to."

"When, Alan? When do you want me?"

"Any time. Tuesday, Wednesday, Thursday."

"I'll come Tuesday. I'll meet you anywhere you say on Tuesday," Vannie's voice was passionate and desperate as they moved away.

I must have a talk with Vannie, I thought, and as I sang to the child I went over in my mind the things that I would say. No harder speech could be imagined for she was Mag's child after all, and not mine. What right had I to interfere in the life of someone else's daughter? Yet what right had I not to interfere?

> I'll not marry you nor the President,
> M hmmm, M hmmm.
> I'll not marry you nor the President,
> Without old Uncle Rat's consent——

I stopped my song and the baby did not move, so I put him on the pallet beside the sleeping Bob, then I tiptoed back to the living room in search of Vannie. I saw her there standing against the wall, and Alan came in soon after. The dance was over and another set was formed. Alan chose the Houston girl and Ben Wheeler danced with Vannie.

Rufus Wells was not dancing. He stood by the door as I came out. Our eyes met but the magic was gone now. We looked at each other and turned away, ashamed. The lamps on the wall flared up and smoked the chimney each time the door opened to let in a gust of wind. Once the flame went out and I lifted the chimney carefully from the bottom to light it again.

"Some day I'm going to hang a wagon wheel on a chain

from that high ridge pole and have candles there, out of the way of the door," I remarked, to have something to say.

"You don't want an old wagon wheel hanging over your head," Rufus said with a smile. "Wagon wheels ought to be used for wagons and nothing else."

"How about an ox bow, with lanterns hanging from two curved ends?"

Still he shook his head and his grey eyes smiled.

"Ox bows are what you yoke oxen with and not for holding lanterns. Tomorrow I'll make you something out of iron, round or curved, whichever way you want it, but it'll not be made for anything else but to hold light."

It was the craftsman who loved his craft that was speaking. Now we could look at each other and laugh together and no longer feel ashamed. Our friendship was back where it was in the beginning. We danced again, but it was not the same as our first dance together. Lizzie danced too, no longer looking back with an embarrassed smile toward the other women sitting on the benches.

By the stars and the moon, we knew it was late, but no one showed any sign of going home. I boiled coffee in the big pressure cooker and the old folks came into the kitchen to drink it from saucers or cups or plates. The fiddlers paused to rest and there were play party games to take the place of dancing. The more religious ones could join in, for there was no fiddle music with it. The young couples promenaded in and out and sashayed up and down the room in the same dance steps, but to the music of their own voices. I could hear Alan's voice above all the others. I tried to see him with Vannie's eyes. He was handsome, with his dark hair falling over his forehead, and there was a slight dimple in his chin. Still, I thought, I like the grey eyes best, and Bill Wells came into my mind.

Dawn came and the play party games and the dancing to fiddle music went on, with no sign of stopping. Now and then a young boy cut a shine, dancing a jig alone with his steps keeping lively time to the music. More of the older women had gone off to sleep with the children across the beds or on pallets. Two young boys who had drunk more raw whiskey than their stomachs could take, began to quarrel and drew out their knives to fight. Rufus Wells parted them and sent them sternly away. The sun rose high and we blew out the lamps. The cow came back to her calf and the chickens flew down from their perch and flocked to the chicken yard gate, impatiently waiting for their food. At last the guests began to depart, and each one said, upon leaving, "You'd best come on home with me."

It was noon, with the sun slant from the south door pointing in a straight line, when the last one took his leave and drove off in a wagon drawn by mules. I went to my room to roll up the pallets, and on the floor, where Bob had slept, I saw a folding pocketknife that had fallen from his pocket.

"I found it," Bob said, coming into the room. "I found it out of doors."

"Does a knife really mean so much to you, Bob?" I groaned.

"Well, I found it."

How could I change with words these children, who had come to me only that year with characters that had been formed by circumstances far back in their early childhood? Sermons would not take away Mag's indifference to her daughter, nor Jeff's shiftlessness, nor Granny's blood in her veins, nor would they take away the years when Bob and his brother had to shift for themselves and take their food where they could find it. I could only take them as they were, and go on from there.

"We'll go down to the valley and ask Uncle George if he knows whose it is," I said, putting the knife away in my room. "Perhaps on Tuesday we'll go."

We slept a great part of that day, for we were tired from the excitement and lack of sleep. I said nothing to Vannie. It was better, I decided, to let her fight her battle alone. There was a struggle going on inside her, which could be seen in her face. If she won that struggle of her own accord, it would make the future easier for her.

On Tuesday morning she cleared her throat to speak, and then she changed her mind and said nothing. She took out the blue muslin dress that she loved, hesitated, then she put it back in the drawer.

"Vannie," I said, "that old rose silk dress of mine you thought was so pretty. Let's get it out and make it over to fit you, today."

Her face lit up, and we started for the dress. Then she hesitated again, and cleared her throat to speak.

"I was just thinking, maybe I'll go down to the valley to-day," she said. "Mamma—all that work she's got to do—she needs help maybe."

"You don't need to. I was aiming to go down myself this morning," Granny spoke up.

I held the rose silk dress up to measure it on Vannie. She looked at herself in the mirror, with her cheeks flushed the color of the dress.

"It'd be a sight better for you to stay on here and sew that

dress than to go down to whatever it is you're up to,"
Granny went on.

I motioned for her to keep quiet, but the damage was
done. I saw a defiant look come into Vannie's eyes.

"Anyhow, I'm going," she said, putting the dress aside.
"I've been gone from home a long time without staying
with the folks."

"We'll all go, then," I said. "Today's as good a day as any
to take that knife down to Uncle George's."

Vannie looked at me quickly. She suspected Granny and
me. We were trying to keep her away from Alan and she
was more determined to go than ever. The battle was on,
but it was not a battle of words. We spoke of commonplace
things, but we knew what the other was thinking. If only
Granny hadn't spoken, I thought. She was winning the battle herself. Now we had to keep her back by force.

"I'll set the table by the fireplace to have it ready when
you come back," she said.

"No, never mind. I've decided to turn the cow in with the
calf and let the pig and chickens out to forage in the woods
for their food, so we can spend the night there, too," I
replied.

"Why can't I keep the knife?" Bob pleaded. "I found it,
I tell you. What you find is yours to keep."

"Not if you find the owner, too."

It was easy to point a moral lesson to Bob.

Alan came that morning as we were talking, and neither
Vannie nor I won. He was the winner. He came in and sat
with us, and he talked of trivial things in that maddening
way of one who has something to say and is waiting for the

right time to say it. Vannie watched him, her face a study in
two expressions, one of joy at seeing him and one of dread
at what he might have come to say. At last it was out.

"I'm on my way back home," he said.

"For good?" Vannie asked, astonished.

"Yes, for good, I reckon. Made up my mind it's about
time to go home."

"Seems like Vannie's made up her mind to the same
thing," Granny spoke up.

"We'll miss you," I said, quickly interrupting her.

I was grateful it had turned out his way. But it seemed a
cruel way to me. It would have been better for Vannie if
she had been the one to decide against the meeting. It would
have given her a feeling of triumph, and courage for other
battles.

"I aimed to go down to the valley today," Vannie said
shyly, as if to remind him of something he might have forgotten. "I thought maybe I might see you there."

"No. You'd have found me gone," he said.

After a pause in which no one could find words, he got up.

"Guess I'd better be on my way. I'll hike over to the
Cherry Hill road and maybe I can pick up a ride there."

We heard him whistling as he walked through the woods
to the Cherry Hill road.

"Well, come on," Granny said. "Everybody's been talking
so hard about going down to the valley today. Let's get
started."

She left us at Uncle George's post office, and went on her
way home, but Vannie stayed with me.

"By God," Uncle George said when I gave him the knife

and asked him to find the owner, "if the boy's so set on a knife, I'll give him one."

But Bob suffered that day from the discipline I had failed to use with Vannie.

"No, that's no way for him to get one," I said. "I'll think of some other way, later."

Chapter XVII

VANNIE found a hairpin and hung it on a pine tree to bring her a letter, but no letter came. She watched for falling stars and red birds that flew up to higher branches and turkey buzzards that flapped their wings, to make a secret wish. But the wish I know she made did not come true. No word came from Alan and we did not see him again. Now her only song was "Twenty-one years, babe, is a mighty long time." She sang it as she worked and she sang it when we went out for a walk in the woods. Even Bob and I found ourselves humming and whistling it, for the tune stayed in our heads and we could not get it out.

Winter came suddenly. The temperature dropped, as it so often does in our part of the country, from seventy degrees down to ten above zero within forty-eight hours. We built roaring fires and huddled close to keep warm. We saw few people then, for the ride in an open wagon was cold, and no one passed for days at a time.

We read from the sets of George Eliot and Charles Dickens that we had on the shelves, and we found ourselves looking upon the characters as real people. We had no patience with characters weakly drawn. They must stand out plainly for us to know, as Uncle George and Jock Wheeler and Granny Massery did. Our friends of the valley were far away. We must walk ten miles over frozen ground, with a cold wind blowing against us, to be with them. Only once a week we saw them, and the rest of the time they were shadows, living in our memories as David Copperfield did, or Silas Marner and little Eppie. We spoke of the people in books the same way as we spoke of those in the valley.

"He didn't have to stay on and take what he did from that old stepfather. Reckon why he didn't run away?" Bob said once of David Copperfield.

And Vannie worried much over Ada and Richard in *Bleak House*.

"She ought to have married him sooner, even if that old Jarndyce didn't want her to," she said. "Maybe Richard wouldn't have died then."

We found more and more pleasure in reading about what people ate, for food was becoming important to us. When we read of meat roasted over a bed of coals on a string, with the heat turning it around, dropping its grease in a pan on the hearth, we roasted a chicken that way. It tasted good, as only food eaten in hunger can taste.

Our food supply began to dwindle. Vannie had been right. The jars of tomatoes and corn and beans were empty now, and we were nearing the end of the whippoorwill peas and sweet potatoes. There were still blackberries. Three times a day we had them, in a cobbler or a pie, or plain with cream poured over them. We had long ago forgotten the hours we had spent picking and canning them.

Our morning prayer came to have a new meaning when we said, "Give us this day our daily bread."

The animals began to suffer from hunger, too. The sudden cold had killed the mountain grass, and even the dry, dead blades were covered from time to time with snow. The cow gave less milk and the chickens, without green food and the worms and grasshoppers of summer, laid no more eggs. They followed me about whenever I stepped out of the house, with hungry eyes searching for scraps of food to be given them. But there were no scraps from our table any more. Even our gluttonous Adolphus, who managed to get food when there was food to be had, was growing lean, and she squealed impatiently whenever she saw me. She was the first one to go.

One morning when she followed us, grunting hungrily all the way to the post office, Jock Wheeler called out, "You ought to kill that hog. She's running herself gaunt, going loose like that."

But even Bob had said it would be like eating Zozo or the cat to eat this animal that had insisted on becoming a pet against our wishes. I could not breed her and feed a big litter as well as herself, so I traded her to Jock Wheeler for a wagon load of cotton seed and corn, for the cow and chickens. The last days of Adolphus were spent in a pen, feasting to her heart's content, and rolling contentedly in the dirt, grunting happily.

The Indians called February the Lean or Hungry month. Now everyone felt the pinch of poverty. Some suffered more than others. The Masserys had as little to eat as we, for February was always a hungry month to them. Jeff Massery talked about going away to some town where he could get a job and earn a regular wage, but he made no move to leave. The thrifty ones had canned enough in other summers to see them through this year of drouth. But the little money they had earned from their cash crops was almost gone.

"If it comes down to it, I'd as soon wear overalls made out of tow sacks," Jock Wheeler said. "But derned if I'd like it when I have to eat cornbread for breakfast."

Rufus Wells' iron shoe last was passed around from house to house, to mend shoes that were fast wearing out, and more patches were added to overalls and coats and dresses. Babies had croup and old folks came down with influenza and pneumonia, and old Doctor Pearce was called from the settlement beyond the valley to stay with first one and then the other, whoever needed him most. Each night, the valley people went somewhere, to sit up with the sick.

There was poverty and want and hunger all about us. The deer came up from the narrows, nibbling at the dry oak leaves, still clinging stubbornly to the trees, and finding little nourishment there. Squirrels scurried about in the cold, searching for nuts and acorns hidden away in places they had forgotten, and possums lay in hollow logs trying to sleep the winter away. We felt closer, then, to all creatures with a will to live.

When the corn and cotton seed were gone, I began to sell the chickens. Every week we took down two of them, carrying them in sacks across our shoulders, bumping against our backs with each step we took.

"Look here, you'll not have enough left for laying," Uncle George warned me.

He banded the chickens he bought from me and let them run with his own instead of keeping them in pens to take to town when he went. He sold me corn meal with the money they brought. I boiled corn meal mush for the dog, fed corn meal mixed with water to the remaining chickens and gave the cow a little to stand still while we milked her. And I in-

vented more ways to cook corn meal for our table than I
thought possible. We had Southern spoon bread, tamale loaf,
gumbo with corn meal instead of rice when there were
scraps of squirrel or rabbit left over from a stew, and mush
sliced and fried.

I felt the weight of the whole world on me then. Everything demanded its very existence of me. Surely, I thought,
even the sun could not rise without me, nor the sap come up
in the trees. I felt the responsibility of the universe, with
everything in it depending on me.

There was no more money. When the last dollar was
spent I felt a strange sense of relief. At last the thing I had
dreaded so long had come. The worst had happened, and
there was nothing more to dread, nothing more to lie awake
and worry about at night. But that kind of relief cannot
last long.

We had no kerosene for the lamps and we threw pine
knots in the fire to light the room, and slivers of rich pine
burned in a bucket lid on the table. They flared up quickly
and went out, and we had to replace them often, one after
the other. I did not want to go to bed early. By such light as
I had, I lost myself in reading long after the others were
asleep.

Sometimes we had meat, squirrel or rabbit or possum, or
fish from the creek. Ben Wheeler came often to borrow my
gun, and he shared the game with us, and when we went
out for our walks in the woods, our treasure hunts were for
the flesh of animals. We cooked the food in an iron skillet
on the hearth to get all the sustenance, the scraps were used
in gumbo and tamales, and the bones were boiled to make a
broth. But more often we had only corn meal and black-

berries to eat. Then our supply of these began to dwindle.

One morning, early, I saw a young deer standing alert beyond the rose garden, looking quickly this way and that, his
dainty feet poised, ready to leap at any sign of danger. My
first instinct was to stay hidden from his view, admiring his
beauty and graceful movements, and I pitied the hunger
that drove him so close to the house. Bob's footsteps sounded
in the kitchen as he got up from his cot, and the deer, like
a trained dancer, gave a leap over the bushes, and was off in
the narrows before I could blink an eye. When I could no
longer see him, the old instinct of self-preservation came
back. I was hungry and I wanted his flesh.

"I saw a deer going toward the narrows," I said, and I
took down the rifle that hung over the door.

Bob jumped into his clothes in less time than I have ever
known, and we could hear Vannie scurrying about in her
room to join us. It was not the hunting season, but I was in
no mood then to be told when I could or could not be hungry and feed hungry mouths dependent on me. Those laws
were made by men in the cities, who came out to hunt, not
because they needed meat, but because it gave them pleasure
to kill. We had passed their camps in our walks, after the
short season was over, and once we saw the carcasses of eight
deer, rotting, with buzzards flying away at our approach to
hover near until we went away. The men had killed more
than they could take back with them, and they left them for
the buzzards and bobcats to feast upon. Zozo enjoyed it,
but it sickened us.

We lost the tracks of the deer we stalked, for they were
so faint upon the hard ground, and we retraced our steps
and looked all around, to see which direction he had taken.

The snow fell against our faces and the wind slapped at us and tore our hair. Bob's toes were coming out of his shoes, for they were beyond mending, and I felt the cold for him.

"Look! Yonder behind the persimmon shoots," Vannie whispered.

I saw something brown, the color of the dry oak leaves, move slightly behind the bare, close-growing bushes. Bob, in his excitement, stepped forward and a twig broke under his feet. In the stillness it was like a sudden explosion. A head reared up, with the tinkle of a bell, and two brown eyes stared at me.

"It's the sorrel mare," I said, still whispering, though there was no longer any need to.

"There's something on the ground with her," Bob said, carefully creeping toward her.

She did not move at our approach, but stood still, watching our every move.

"It's a colt, a newborn colt, and it's not a mule colt either," Bob shouted excitedly.

A little brown foal, so newly born it was still wet and panting, with something I took to be the birth sac on the ground beside it, rose, struggling, to its feet. Its long legs were so stiff we thought they would surely break if they were ever bent again. It turned around and stared at Bob, with soft eyes of dark blue. Bob stared back, speechless, unable to move.

The foal had come into a cold, damp world. The dead grass under its feet bowed low in the wind and the bare trees shuddered and moaned as if in pain. But pale little leaf buds on the persimmon shoots were beginning to swell, woodpeckers tapped hopefully at a sweetgum tree, and down at the creek we heard the first faint trill of a toad. Soon, when its eyes were clear, a new-made world would appear for him to look upon.

We gave up our search for the deer and turned our steps toward home, to a breakfast of corn meal mush and blackberries.

"It—it looked at me," Bob said with awe. "I was the first thing it saw. Before even it saw the mare, it looked at me."

I had started to write an article when I first came to Rocky Crossing, before I knew the people well. Later, at harvest time, I revised it and added to it. Now I took it out and finished it, and when we went down to the valley, I addressed it to a New York magazine and gave it to Uncle George to mail.

"It's to go first class," I said.

"Hell, you don't send packages first class," he replied.

"But this has writing in it. Writing goes first class."

"Printing don't. What's the difference between writing and printing, I'd like to know," he went on.

"I can't pay you for the stamps," I said.

I thought of the words he had said when I first came here. The government bets you a passel of land against your time, you'll not stick it out for three years. The government was close to winning that bet with me, but I was not ready to give up yet. There was one thing left to do.

"Uncle George," I said, "in about a year and a half I'll have title to my land, and the timber will be mine. I'd like to mortgage that timber to you for enough to see me through till then."

Uncle George struck a match on the metal button of his

overalls and lit his pipe. He puffed, with his cheeks like bellows, until it caught.

"I'd not be able to keep a store here if folks didn't come to buy on credit," he said. "What do you think would happen if I never sold a thing except when there was cash money around? They'd all be going in to town to do their trading and I'd have to close up. Now you don't need to worry, I'll not lose by your trade, and I can wait on the money till the timber's sold without any mortgages."

I bought the flour and sugar that I needed and tea and kerosene. Uncle George took some cans of peaches, corn beef and tomatoes from a shelf.

"I went and stocked up on stuff like this when you first came here because this is what you used to buy. Now they're a loss to me, gathering dust on the shelves. I'd be beholden if you'd take them off my hands."

I took what we could carry on our backs, and the rest was left to be brought up the hill by the first wagon that would be passing that way. We stopped at the Wells home to warm by their fire. Lizzie was in the front bedroom, taking stitches on a quilt that hung by ropes from the ceiling on a wooden frame. We put down our bundles and sat on the chairs she brought in from the kitchen. Vannie and I stitched with her while we rested. Bob was still filled with awe and wonder at the newborn foal that we had seen. Rufus came into the room and he tried to tell him about it.

"We saw the colt—" he began. "It looked at me before it saw its own mother."

He had no words to tell of the way he felt. He could only grope and nothing else came but, "I was the first thing in all the world it saw, and we almost shot it for a deer."

Rufus looked at me. I had expected him to tease because we were hunting out of season, but his grey eyes were serious. He started to speak, but changed his mind. Instead he picked up the baby from his pallet and rocked his straight chair backward and forward.

On a night soon after I heard the sound of footsteps in my sleep. They came to the house and the door softly opened, then there was the sound of their going away again. I turned over on my pillow. It was something I had dreamed, I thought. Hens cackling and bumble bees humming could seem like human voices in my sleep, and Zozo or the pattering feet of a squirrel or a fox were like human footsteps coming to visit me. But when I awoke the next morning, I saw some venison in a burlap bag on the floor. Often after that there was game left silently inside the door.

The Widow Johnson passed in her wagon on the way to visit her sister in town, and she brought the supplies I had bought, from the valley. She looked at the magazines on the shelf in the living room, and she picked one up to examine it.

"Now if my boys could have something like this around the house, it'd make them want to read and learn their lessons better," she said.

I offered them to her.

"I'm glad to find a place for them, for they are accumulating so here I haven't any more room on the shelves," I said.

"I'll not take them without a trade," she said. "I've jars of corn and snap beans and wild plums to spare, more than ever we need. I'll trade that for them."

So we made the trade, magazines that I did not need for food she did not need. And I made another trade . . . I let

Ben Wheeler have my rifle in exchange for part of the game he hunted.

These were the poor whites, the Wheelers, the Nixons, the Wells and the Widow Johnson, people who live in unpainted shacks and go barefoot in the summer, who wear patched clothes and smell of sweat and tobacco and cotton cloth. In some states they are called "Peckerwoods" or "Crackers." Cartoons are drawn about them and plays are written about them to make people laugh. But I lived through the rest of that winter, knowing a kindness and a generosity I had never known before, when, in their poverty, they shared the little they had with me and among themselves.

Chapter XVIII

WE WAITED all winter for a miracle, and the miracle that came was spring. Even the weeds were beautiful to us, rising up from the earth, jade green, glistening in the sun, with splashes of yellow and blue of the dog's-tooth and bird's-foot violets. The trees were like young girls in dainty new party dresses, holding out their arms to primp and pose before the tall, dark pines. We could forgive Nature now for all that had passed. We could even say it was our fault and not hers. We might have worked a little harder, hoeing to give the roots more air, terracing with rocks to hold the moisture in the soil, watching more closely the bugs and worms that crawled over the leaves.

Once more Daddy Means plowed the land for us, and once more we planted the seeds with high hopes. We planted four seeds to each one of last year, one for the rabbits, one for the bugs, one for the drouth and one for us. We could almost see them rise out of the ground after a light, warm rain. Our hands were not too dainty now for any kind of work, nor our backs too proud to bear any load. We gathered fertilizer from the woods where the herds of cows and mules had roamed, and brought it back in burlap bags to our plants. And we dug rich soil from the creek bottom to enrich the whole garden. Every weed was hoed away and the rows were kept clean. There was room enough in the rest of the forest for the wild flowers. The cat helped, too, by keeping steady watch for rabbits that came in the night.

The hens found bugs and worms and tender shoots of grass and they began to lay again, and they hid their nests in the brush with the quail, to raise new broods of chickens. We borrowed another cow from Uncle George when the brindle one went dry and her calf was weaned. And we had our first poke sallet of the season, cooked with green onions and scrambled eggs, and radishes with sweet butter. We had come through the winter. We'd win that bet yet with the government. And the sale of the timber would pay our debt to Uncle George.

We had not been conscious of the labor we had done to build the rose garden. A few rocks added to the wall, more flat stones for the path and planting now and then flowers and low-growing bushes that we dug up from the woods, had not been work to us. But when the roses bloomed, with the azaleas and wild irises bordering them, in all their glory, the garden seemed to have appeared suddenly before us, like something Aladdin had wished for with a rub of his lamp. We had our afternoon lessons there, with the west wind blowing petals over us, and dropping them at our feet.

Bob and Vannie read aloud as I lay on the grass to listen, and to tell them the meaning of words they stumbled over. From where I lay, I could see things I had not seen from higher up, a black cricket hopping through the flowers, an ant carrying a heavy burden as it walked over a grass blade, a pale green katydid like a leaf moving. I had seen things from the bottom that winter, in another way, things I would never have seen from higher up. I could look back now and call it a magnificent experience, one I would not have wanted to miss, but which I hoped never to have again.

We heard a faint tinkle of bells, and Bob dropped his book.

"Mule bells!" he exclaimed, and he was off in a flash, a streak of blue overalls dashing through the forest, with the spotted dog running excitedly behind him.

I had given up trying to hold him back when he heard the bells of the wandering herds. Sometimes he would be gone for hours, and sometimes he came back soon, with a disgusted air, saying, "Nothing but the cows."

He followed the sorrel mare all over the mountain side, only to gaze at a distance upon her colt, for the creatures were too wild to allow him to come near. I had once worried about him when the hours passed and he did not return. But now I knew he was somewhere, looking wistfully at a little brown colt that pranced and played at its mother's side, and I knew, too, that I would not see him again until hunger drove him back.

We could hear his shouts down the road even before he turned the bend and came in sight.

"I saw him! I saw him!"

His eyes shone and his face was flushed. He was exhausted from following the herd, but too excited to know how tired he was. He sat down to his supper and forgot to eat.

"He's getting so big now, you wouldn't believe a colt could grow so fast."

He took a bite of soufflé and drank some milk.

"He knows me. I'm certain sure he knows me for he looks me square in the eye like he did the day he was born, and he points his ears at me. That means he likes me and he's glad to see me. That means he's not afraid."

The days were warm enough to go down to the creek again. Bob stood behind a tree to take off his overalls and he threw them toward us to be washed. Then we saw a streak of white running around the bend, followed by a splash in the water, with shouts and a whistle, and the happy bark of the dog.

The old intimacy the creek had given us came back as Vannie and I waded out in the water to rub soap on the clothes to make them white.

"That time the Widow Johnson came by in the wagon," Vannie said. "Just that morning I saw a turkey buzzard and I made a wish. 'I wish something nice would happen,' I said, and it flopped its wings and I knew the wish was coming true."

Three months had passed since Alan left and she had not heard from him. Still she could look upon it as something nice that happened on the day she first met him. I thought of Bill Wells. Soon he would be coming home to help his father with the crops until time to go off to some college where a poor boy could work his way through. I was sorry he had not been the first to appear on that hot summer day when she was wishing for something nice to happen. We took off our dresses that we wore and stood deep in the water to wash them. Suddenly Bob appeared before us.

"I saw a striped bass!" he shouted. "I tried to catch it with my hands for our dinner but I couldn't."

"Wait, Bob," I called, ducking down in the water.

Vannie was on the bank hanging the clothes on a bush, and she could not hide.

"Go back! Go back!" she screamed, covering her small breasts with her hands.

"Aw, I wasn't looking," Bob said, disgusted with women because they had so many parts to hide. He disappeared under the water with only ripples to show where he had been, and a splash later on to show where he went.

Our steps led us often to the creek, sometimes only to bathe, and sometimes to fish. We fried the perch and bass that we caught over a campfire and ate it there on the banks, sitting on a quilt spread on the ground, with the sun making a dappled pattern through the trees about us.

The water rose and fell with the spring rains, sometimes spreading out beyond its banks, leaving deposits of twigs and leaves far out over the ground, and in a short time it was sluggish and low again, like a lazy snake winding slowly on its way.

I could not look upon rain without giving silent thanks, after the summer that had passed. We put on our oldest clothes to walk down to the valley and let the rain fall gently on us, trickling down our hair and eyelashes to our cheeks. Little puddles formed behind us where our footprints had been.

The hairpins Vannie had hung on pine trees, the news bees that circled around us, and the doves that flew over our roof top, brought a message at last, but it was for me and not for her.

"Got a wish book for you," Uncle George said, giving me a Sears, Roebuck catalog. "Here's two," and he gave me one from Montgomery Ward, also. "By God, I get paid for mail that goes out of here and not for what comes in. Nothing ever goes out, and look at all this stuff coming in I've got to

handle, wish books, almanacs, *Kansas City Farm Journal.*
Here's a letter, too, for you, from New York and it's written
on a typewriter."

He waited for me to open it, curious to know what was in
it. It was from the editor of the magazine that had the
article I had written and mailed that winter. And in it
there was a check. I had not believed I would ever see again
as much money as the amount written on it. It was, I suppose, the minimum price paid for a first story. Perhaps even
the editor thought it was a small price to pay. But at the
scale I had been living, spending less than a hundred dollars
a year for all of us, it was enough to pay my debts and live
a long time after.

"Can you cash this check, Uncle George?" I asked with
as much composure as I could force upon myself.

There was no one else in the store but Bob. Even Savannah
had left us to go down to see her people. Uncle George
took the check and looked at it. Then he put on his glasses
and looked again.

"Hell, I've never had that much money in the place all at
one time in my life," he said. "Who's sending you that
much money, anyway?"

He read aloud the whole check, from the date down to the
signature.

"It's what I earned from the magazine article I wrote and
mailed from here," I said.

"You mean they paid you this much just for writing
something?" he asked. "By God, don't let Jeff Massery know
you can get money that easy. He'll be using up all the paper
and pencils I've got on the place."

I didn't tell Uncle George that writing was not easy, that

it was more than pushing pencils over blank sheets of paper. I had thought that he, more than all the others, would understand.

"I'll take it to town, then, in the next wagon going that way," I said, when he gave the check back to me.

Now I could buy flour and sugar and canned peaches on credit without a feeling of shame and defeat, for there was money waiting to pay for them. I could buy all I needed and things I did not need.

That winter we had gone without necessities, a light in the night to read by, warm clothes to keep out the cold, and at times there was not even enough food to eat. Luxuries were so far beyond my reach that they became a symbol to me. I forgot the food and warmth I needed. There was nothing I wanted more then than sweet-smelling bath salts, a soft fur neckpiece, or ice cream in the summertime.

"Reckon you'll be like all the others," Uncle George said as he put the things I had bought in the burlap bag. "Reckon now you've got cash money, you'll be going to town to spend it."

We laughed about it, for that was exactly what I intended to do.

"I'll be going in the very next wagon that passes Rocky Crossing," I answered.

Uncle George was still bewildered, but he was a little proud of me.

"Those chickens you brought down here last winter," he said. "I've still got them, for I figured some day you'd want them back. How'd you like me to send them to you in the next wagon going that way?"

Our packs were not heavy to us as we walked home that

day, and the road seemed no longer steep and far. We stopped on the way and ate peppermint candy we had bought, and gave some to the Wells children who came running out to the gate to meet us. And we made our plans for a trip to town.

Chapter XIX

THE cow, waiting by the calf lot, began to moan, and the sound was taken up by one of the herds passing through. Vannie said it was a sign of high water. It had rained all night, and daylight came, cloudy and dripping, without the sun. We could hear the waters of the creek rushing with a sound like rumbling thunder. A wagon came down the road from the direction of the valley, and we pressed our faces to the window to see who it could be. It was not a day for traveling anywhere.

Jock Wheeler came in sight, with his wife and son on the wagon seat beside him, sheltered under a large umbrella, and they stopped at the gate.

"You'll never make the crossing," I called out. "Better stay on here till the water's down."

Young Ben unhitched the mules and took them to the calf lot, then he followed his parents into the house. They were on their way to the county seat, they said, to buy seed corn, for they had used all theirs for food last winter. They stayed three days with us. The rain clouds passed and the sun came out again, but the creek was still high. Bob and Ben went out, like Noah's dove, several times a day to let us know what the waters were doing.

"I'm bound to be getting on," Uncle Jock said, restlessly. "That corn's due to go in the ground now."

He knew of a place in the woods where we might ford the creek. We put on our best clothes and went with them, sitting with Ben on a quilt in the bed of the wagon. The mules wove in and out between the trees until we came to the rushing, roaring creek. Jock got down and tested its depth with a stick. Gently and slowly he and Ben led the mules in, one on each side to hold the reins. The water gradually swallowed their feet, their knees, their thighs, until at last all we could see ahead of us were their heads and shoulders, and the long necks of the mules stretched high. We climbed in the seat beside Mrs. Wheeler, who held the reins, with a taut face turned toward her husband and son in the water. We could feel the wagon bumping over the rough bed of the creek. The water seeped up to the wagon, slapping against our feet. Through the loud noise of the water we could hear Jock's voice talking calmly to his mules, "Easy now, Babe. Come on, Sal. All right. That's all right. Just a little more and we'll be over."

The waves were like long fingers reaching out to clutch at them and drag them in. Were they swimming, I wondered, or were their feet on the rocks? And could the mules hold on? At last we reached the other bank, but that was steep and slippery. Again Jock coaxed in gentle tones that one uses to calm a frightened child. One of the mules slipped back into the water and the wagon jerked as if it were being torn from the shafts. Water sprayed over us and we felt ourselves pulling with the waves. It was Jock's own will power that got the mule back on her feet, and up the steep, clay bank.

The trees and brush were too close together on the other side for the wagon to pass. The boys walked ahead to make a path for us. They bent down the saplings in the way, and Bob sat on them to hold them down while Ben cut the slender trunks with his pocketknife, bit by bit.

When we reached the wagon trail at last, we sat back and sighed. Jock and Ben and Bob walked beside the wagon until their clothes were dry. A rabbit ran across our path, and hid from our sight.

"A sign of bad luck for sure," Mrs. Wheeler said. "Whenever you see a rabbit in your path, you'd best turn around and go home to start over again, or you'll have bad luck all the way."

"About the worst luck I could think of happening to me would be to cross that creek again and go back home," Jock Wheeler said without slowing his pace.

"I'll turn my hat around. That'll fool the rabbit and make him think we're going back," Ben said.

We took off our hats and put them on backward and rode on our way. When we came to a hill, we got out to lighten the load, and we pushed the wagon to help the mules along. Zozo trotted with us then, but at the top of the hill she jumped up when she saw us get back in. Jock, so tender and gentle with his mules in the deep water, yelled as we went bouncing and bumping down the hill, "Whoa, there, Babe. Get on there, Sal, you sorry old thing. Why don't you keep up?"

When the sun was directly overhead, we stopped by the side of the road to eat the lunch I had prepared, and to let the mules rest and graze, but we did not linger long, for we had far to go.

It took us fifteen hours to travel the thirty-five miles from our house to the county seat. The little stores around the courthouse square were dark when we arrived at last, and only here and there did we see a light shining from the windows of some houses where people were sitting up late. The Wheelers had friends living in town and they stopped overnight with them, but we went to the only hotel there. It was a yellow frame boarding house, set behind an iron picket fence, with two old magnolias in full bloom towering above it. They gave us one room to sleep in and we felt stifled in it, with the walls and ceilings too tightly plastered. We raised the long windows as far as we could to let in the air, and we gazed out in the darkness at the shadows of houses around us. We were like excited children on Christmas Eve, eagerly waiting for morning to come.

Our county seat is small, with a population of less than two thousand, but it was like a metropolis to me, coming there after more than a year away from towns and cities. The children clung to me that next morning as we walked down the streets that faced the square. There were more wagons than automobiles parked around the courthouse square, and more men in overalls and women in homemade cotton dresses, than those in town clothes. But I was bewildered at seeing so many strange faces and hearing strange voices speaking to others and not to me. An automobile passed and the soft voice of a woman sang out, but we could see only a fat, gruff man sitting at the wheel alone. It was so funny that we looked at each other and laughed, though we knew the voice came from a radio in the car.

It was good to hear music again, and I stopped before a little lunchroom to listen to the radio there. I had not real-

ized how much I missed it until then. There had been music
of the wilderness, with the movements and rhythms of the
seasons. Now, in a few minutes as I stood on the sidewalk
listening, I could have all the seasons and all the moods
coming to me at once, the soft clear notes of early spring
with bird songs and flute calls of frogs, and the staccato
notes of the woodpecker. Then the languid, sensuous music
of summer, with the purring of the pines and the low running creek and the murmur of bees and insects, rising
higher and louder to a crescendo of the moans and shrieks
of a storm, with drum roars of thunder. The lull followed,
that comes after a storm, with the call of birds again and
the whisper of trees, and the music was over. I felt as if I
had lived through all the seasons while I stood there.

Bob and Vannie wandered off to look at the shop windows. I left them waiting for me while I went into the
bank to deposit my check. Banks were safe now, I had been
told. The time was past when a depositor could lose his
whole life's savings overnight through someone else's dis-
honesty or carelessness. Bob was still staring in the same
window when I came out, looking at a display of pocket-
knives. He did not have to "find" one now, to be taken
away from him and returned to Uncle George. He could
have one of his very own, to keep.

"Which do you like best?" I asked.

He chose a fancy knife with several blades, one that could
be used as a spoon, one as a nail file, and three that were
sharp for cutting. While I was buying it, Vannie walked
over to look at dresses. Through the window I saw a bus
stop to take on passengers for Little Rock. I felt reckless
then. First Little Rock and then the world! We'd buy a

pretty new dress and go to the city to pleasure ourselves. We'd go to a real hotel with bellboys and elevators and we'd eat in a restaurant with men in white jackets to wait on us, and we'd hear a concert or see a movie. The Wheelers could take the animals down to the valley and look after them for us. There was no need to hurry home.

Vannie looked at the price tag on a white dotted Swiss dress trimmed with Irish lace. She picked up the ticket and dropped it as if it had burned her hands.

"Seventeen dollars and forty-nine cents for just one dress," she whispered to me in a bewildered voice. "We could make us a dozen dresses for seventeen dollars and forty-nine cents."

She was the little old lady again, wiser than I, as she walked to the piece goods and pattern department and chose white dotted Swiss and Irish lace by the yard. I heard a motor start and the bus went on its way to Little Rock without us. I watched till it was out of sight, then I turned to buy material for other dresses, and overalls, shirts and sturdy shoes for Bob. As a compromise, there were white shoes and a pair each of silk stockings for Vannie and me, and some lavender perfumed soap and dusting powder.

The sun rose high and warm. Old men came out to loiter in the square, sitting on wooden benches to whittle and to talk. The women wove in and out of the stores, going now and then to old, battered automobiles or to wagons to leave their parcels. There were greetings here and there, of friends who lived far apart, seeing each other at the county seat for the first time in many months, and bits of their conversation came to us as we passed.

We went to the lunchroom when we were through with

our shopping and sat at the counter. The radio was still on, but instead of the music I had stood outside to hear, a woman, or a man, I could not tell which, was singing in a low, moaning voice. It was a new way of singing and it hurt my ears. I wanted the music of the wilderness again, coming to me slowly through the long seasons.

I had seen Vannie's eyes searching here and there all morning, and when she had glanced quickly toward each tall, thin man with dark curly hair that passed, I could almost hear her heart miss a beat. I found myself looking about for Alan, too. But we saw Bill Wells instead when we came out of the lunchroom.

"Hello, Bill," I said, reaching out my hand from the many parcels I carried. "It's good to see you here."

We stood on the sidewalk to talk to him. Bob showed him his knife and opened all the blades, and even Vannie was cordial. If we could happen to see Bill on the street, we might also happen to see Alan, she must have thought. I knew the question that was in her eyes and I asked it for her.

"Have you seen Alan lately?"

Bill was embarrassed, and he hesitated.

"No," he spoke at last. "Alan's gone to Missouri to look for a job."

"What town?" Vannie wanted to know.

"He didn't say. Just said he was going to Missouri to get a job, that's all I know."

There was something about the way he said it that made me think there was something else he knew, but would not tell. Vannie noticed it, and she asked, shyly, "Is he all right?"

"Yes, he's all right," Bill replied, not looking at us as he spoke.

Bob saw the Wheelers coming toward their wagon that stood at the courthouse square, and he shouted out to them. They waved in reply and climbed into the wagon, to wait for us. Vannie and Bob went to join them, putting our packages in the back with the bag of seed corn Jock Wheeler had bought. I turned to Bill to ask what was wrong, but I thought better of it, and said,

"Good-bye. I'll tell your folks that we saw you."

Ben sat in the back with Vannie and Bob and Zozo, and Jock and his wife moved over to make room for me on the seat with them.

"Just found out Alan is going to get married," Ben Wheeler said as we started off. "He's going to marry some girl named Duncan when he comes back from Missouri."

Vannie said nothing. She was absorbed in arranging the packages in the bed of the wagon to make room for her feet. We rode on quietly for a long time, with no other sound but the steps of the mules and the turning of the wheels striking their iron rims against the rocks.

"Lizzie Wells wanted me to get her some bird's-eye cloth and outing flannel," Mrs. Wheeler said to me in a low voice so no one else could hear. "Reckon that means she's expecting?"

"I reckon so," I agreed.

We had started too late to reach home before the next day, but we knew that, once away from the town, there was not a house where we would not be made welcome that night.

"Might as well stop here as anywhere," Jock Wheeler said at dusk.

He pulled the mules to a halt before a little cabin set far back from the road. Mrs. Nixon's cousin lived there, and she came out with her husband to invite us in. They spread a feast for us on the long table in the kitchen. A ham was brought from the smokehouse, and two chickens were killed, and every vegetable that grew in the garden was cooked for us, with white potatoes, sweet potatoes, cornbread and biscuits, and preserves and jellies and relishes to spread on them. Mrs. Wheeler and I lingered on when we had finished, to sit with the woman and her daughters while they ate, and we told them the news of the valley, and of their relatives there.

We slept in one room, some in beds and some on pallets, and we talked until late in the night, when our eyes would stay open no longer. At dawn, after a breakfast as hearty as the supper of the night before, we started on our way.

The water of Rocky Crossing had gone down overnight, and there was a sour smell of damp, dank earth in the shady places. The hoofs of the mules sank deep in the mud, and they stepped high as they walked, like dancing horses in a circus. Small blue butterflies hovered over the stagnant places. One alone was dainty and pretty, but in such a swarm they could be up to no good. I thought of creeping, slimy worms and caterpillars that would come after.

We got out to push the wagon up the hill from the creek, and when we came to the ridge I walked beside the mules. Now I had come to my boundary. It was good to feel my feet on my own land. I hurried my steps, eager to get back home. I had left the calf staked out on a grassy slope, where he could not run away, but where the cow could come to feed him night and morning, and the chicken yard was open so the chickens could get out to forage for their food, as the quails did. They had not suffered by my absence, but they called out a welcome when they heard the wagon approach. And as I turned the bend, I saw my log house behind the stake-an'-rider fence. The two wings were like two arms held out to greet me. No bus to Little Rock could tempt me now.

Chapter XX

THERE was a difference of only three years in Bob's age and Vannie's. But in those three years lay the difference between a child and an adult. When we returned from our long wagon ride to town, Vannie went to her room to put her soap and powder and silk stockings away in the bureau drawer with her other treasures. I could hear her scurrying about, behind the drawn monk's cloth curtains, like a little squirrel searching a burrowing place. Bob lay sprawled on the front door step, testing his knife on a stick, and straining his eyes in the growing dark. He wore his new overalls. When he had emptied the pockets of his old ones, I looked on in dread, for he had seen many things in town that were tempting to a small boy. But there was nothing more than an acorn and a few small rock crystals and stones and part of a deer antler to change from the old pockets to the new.

Bob started to carve his initials on the log wall.

"Bob," I called, hastily.

He picked up his stick again and began to whittle.

"I'm making an arrow," he said. "With my knife and a bow and arrow, I can hunt for our meat."

Before he had the knife, he often eyed the rifle hanging over the door, wistfully hinting to be allowed to use it. Now he went on with his plans for hunting without a gun.

Vannie lit the lamp in her room, and its glow moved from one side of the curtain to the other. She put it on the floor and moved the couch to look under it.

"What's the matter, Vannie?" I called.

"I—I lost something."

"Do you need any help?"

"No."

I rolled Bob's folding cot into the kitchen and spread the sheets on it. And for his bedtime story I told him of David Crockett killing bears in Arkansas on his way to Texas. When I went back to the living room to light the lamp, it was a signal for all the fragile wings of the forest to beat against the screens in search of the flame. The fluttering and tapping of moths and June bugs kept up endlessly, like a persistent knock at the door.

Vannie came in at last, carrying her lamp with her. She held out the wrapper of the chocolate bar Alan had bought her almost a year ago.

"Bob ate my candy," she said. "I found this behind my bed."

Her face was white and the paper rustled in her shaking hand. I knew that her anger was not for Bob alone, but he would be made to suffer for all her pent-up emotions since she had heard the news of Alan's approaching marriage.

"There's no need to wake him now, for the deed is done," I said. "I'll talk to him about it, myself, tomorrow."

I took the lamp from her and put it on the table beside my own, and I unwrapped one of the packages we had brought back with us.

"We'll start cutting on the dotted Swiss tomorrow," I went on. "I think this is a pretty pattern. It's like that dress we saw marked seventeen dollars and forty-nine cents."

A white dress trimmed in Irish lace is a poor substitute, I knew, for laughing eyes and a song and a kiss, but I went on. If she had only exploded in a rage or cried out, I thought, to get some of this out of her system. Instead she had pretended not to hear when Ben Wheeler first told her the news. Now a stale chocolate bar in an empty fruit jar had become a symbol of something which she refused to give up.

We took out the dress goods, ginghams and cotton broadcloth, and looked over the patterns we had bought, making plans of how we would cut and sew them. And I talked of my first party dress and my first beau.

"I thought I couldn't live without him then. Now I've even forgotten his last name," I said.

I glanced up at her as I spoke, but she bent down over the Irish lace in her hand as if she were so intent on studying the pattern, that she had not heard.

"It's funny how things that seem so important come to mean nothing to you later on," I went on.

She did not answer, but her expression said that she would not change, and I spoke no more. Hadn't I felt the same at her age? And would I have let anyone else tell me otherwise then?

The next morning I called Bob to my room.

"Did you take Vannie's candy?" I asked.

He started to deny it, but he saw that was no use.

"Shucks, she didn't aim to eat it. What good did it do her in that old fruit jar?"

I found myself agreeing with him secretly, but I said,

"That's not the point. It belonged to her and not to you. It was up to her to decide what she wanted to do with it."

"Well, anyway, it tasted awful," he went on, as if it made the deed less wrong because he had not enjoyed it.

"Tell me, Bob, when did you take it? Was it before we went down to the post office last Saturday? Before we bought the peppermint candy?"

"Yes. The day before. But it was hard and stale. I didn't even eat it all."

He could see no wrong in what he had done, but because of Vannie he was repentant, and because, no doubt, the candy hadn't been worth stealing after all. I could see the bulge in his pocket that his new knife made. It was the first thing the boy had ever owned in his life, except his clothes that were worn to hide a nakedness which others did not want to see. He had taken the knives and the candy at a time when he thought there was no other way to get what he wanted, just as he had once stolen all the food he ate. Perhaps, with something he could call his own, something nobody could take away from him, he would have respect for the property of others. Even Zozo, who adored him, was my dog and not his. And though he liked to claim the sorrel mare's colt and make believe it was his while he followed it over the mountain side, it belonged to Uncle George's herd. An idea flashed through my mind.

"Bob, how would you like to have the sorrel mare's colt for your own?"

This was not the treatment he had expected for what he had done, and he turned to me with a look in his eyes that said it was a cruel joke.

"We'll talk to Uncle George about it the next time we go down for the mail," I said.

Uncle George and I drove a hard bargain for the colt. No matter how generous or how honest a man is, when it comes to horse trading, the old instinct of getting all you can comes to him. I know I paid more than Uncle George would have taken, but it was less than I was prepared to pay, so we were both satisfied.

Vannie could not understand why Bob should be rewarded because he had stolen from her. I tried to explain that if he had something which he valued very much, he would understand better what it meant to steal.

I wondered how even she could sit so calmly by, taking dainty stitches on her dress without looking up when Uncle George came up the hill after he had rounded up his herd. He led the balky little colt by a rope. It planted its feet on the ground and would not move, then suddenly it jumped and jerked and tried to break away. Uncle George spoke gently and calmly, and even his hells and damns were pleasant enough to calm the animal's fears while we put it in the calf lot. I led the calf to the chicken yard. We would do our milking there so no one but Bob need go near the colt.

Bob stood transfixed, unable to take his eyes off the little creature, and unable, too, to go near and touch it. He had become suddenly shy, and stammered when he tried to talk. Uncle George explained to him how to feed the colt and how to take care of it now that it was taken away from the mother. He stood so still, with his eyes following every movement the animal made, that I thought he had not heard. But he remembered, even to the last detail.

Every morning and every evening he warmed a pan of

skim milk until it was tepid, and he put a little sugar in it, to take out to the lot. He suffered until the colt learned to come of its own accord to bury his nose in the pan, and drink to the last drop. It came to know him at last, and its little ears moved forward with joy to see the boy approach, bringing food and tender words. We sent for some oats by a wagon passing on its way to town, and Bob soaked them in warm water until the colt learned to eat them dry.

Whenever Bob was wanted to bring in wood or water, he could always be found sitting on the fence of the lot, with his eyes following the colt, dreaming, no doubt, of the day when they would be riding, boy and pony merged into one active animal, all over the mountain. Nothing had ever been so completely his own before.

"Vannie ought not to say her prayers like she does," Bob said one morning at the breakfast table.

We looked at him inquiringly.

" 'Cause she don't mean it when she says, 'Forgive us our debts as we forgive our debtors.' "

Vannie cherished her anger and her love, as she cherished the empty fruit jar and the perfumed soap and dusting powder we had brought back from town. I could almost imagine her taking them out now and then and putting them carefully back again in a bureau drawer where she could find them when she wanted them. Bob and I were more alike. We enjoyed what we had when we had it, with no regrets when it was gone.

Gradually he taught the colt to follow where he led, with a rope. They went off together where the grass was green, and Bob lay on the ground, watching as the colt grazed.

One day at noon we heard the sound of a motor on our

road. Automobiles were scarce enough on the dirt highway three miles away, but there was never one on our narrow, winding wagon trail. It could only be coming to our house, because the rocks in the creek were too sharp for tires to cross. Bob had gone out immediately after the noon meal, leading his colt to a grassy clearing. I waited in curiosity until a grey Ford coach drove up and a man got out to walk through the gate. It was the county sheriff. Election was over and there would be no other for more than a year. I invited him in and we talked of the weather and the prospects for a good crop. I knew there was something more he had come to say, but life is unhurried in the mountains, and I waited.

"You got a boy named Bob Jenkins with you here?" he asked at last.

"Yes. He's been here since last summer."

"Well, he's a runaway from the orphanage in Little Rock. They've been trying to find him."

Vaguely I knew that this was what he was going to say. It was as if all this had been acted out before, in some dream or in some other existence, and I was not surprised. When he spoke, it was as if I had heard the words before, and my answers had been given too, in some kind of previous rehearsal.

"He seems happy here. Can't he stay on if I offer him a home here with me?"

"I'm afraid not. He ran away and he'll have to go back. I'm responsible for him now that he's back in this county, for I'm the one that took him there in the first place."

I looked around for Vannie but she was nowhere to be seen, and there were no noises of her stirring about in her room or in the kitchen. I had to think quickly. There was only one way of keeping him, and that was to adopt him. But would an institution approve of sending a child out in the wilderness, far away from schools, churches or doctors? At least I could try.

"Suppose I offer to adopt him?" I asked.

"You'll have to go there and talk to the ones in charge about that. My job is to take him back."

Vannie slipped quietly into the room again like a little grey ghost, and stood beside my chair.

"Have you seen Bob?" I asked.

"No. I've not seen any trace of him. Maybe he's down in the valley," she said.

Hours passed and the sheriff stayed on. Zozo, who had started off with Bob, came back and was playing in the yard, teasing the cat. I knew the boy was not far away, and I knew, too, that he would not return as long as the sheriff remained. I threw out hints, and Vannie lied very calmly, "Maybe he's down in the valley spending the night there." At last I rose and said I must look after the animals for it was their feeding time.

"I'll look around in the valley," the sheriff said, getting up to go. "If he shows up here, I wish you'd send him in with the next one coming that way. As long as he stays in the county, it's my job to take him back."

"If he should go to some other county?" I asked.

"Then, of course, it's no affair of mine."

He grinned when he spoke, and he added, "I've already asked everybody in the valley about him, but nobody had seen hide nor hair of him. And they all looked like this girl here when they said it."

"Neither have you seen hide nor hair of him," I answered.

"I haven't, for a fact, and it looks like I won't. But they're going to hold me responsible as long as he's in my county, though."

I decided that I was going to vote for him in the next election. In the meantime I must think about what to do with Bob.

When the sheriff had gone, and the grey Ford coach had disappeared, Vannie went out again and brought Bob back, leading the colt behind him.

"You promised. You remember you made a promise and you know what happens—" he began when I went out to meet him.

"I know, Bob," I said, and I helped him put the colt in the lot, and closed the gate. We walked back to the house together. "But suppose we just go there to see about adopting you. I'll stay until they let me bring you back home, then nobody can ever make you leave again."

"If you take me back, they'll keep me there. You'll see. And you'll be breaking your promise."

"They can't keep you, Bob, if I say I want to adopt you," I said.

But there was doubt in my voice even as I said the words. Would they let a child go to a place as remote as mine, where he had already gone hungry, and without enough clothes to keep warm in the winter?

"You made a promise," was all that Bob would say. "I won't go back. I'll run away, first."

"All right, Bob. I made you a promise, and I'll keep it."

I thought of the sheriff's words. If he went to some other county, it was no affair of his. Bob had a sister somewhere. He could go and live with her until he was old enough to live where he chose. Uncle George could help me trace her by writing to the postmaster at Ola.

Five days after we went down to speak to him about it, Uncle George came riding to our house on a mule. Bob's sister, he told us, was living on a farm on the main highway, in Yell County, and he gave us her married name.

It was in the early dawn when we walked to the highway with Bob. He wore a new pair of overalls and his sturdy new shoes. His other clothes, and a lunch to eat on the way, were tied in a bundle which he carried over his shoulder on a stick, like the pictures of Christian in our *Pilgrim's Progress*. The little colt trotted behind him, led by a rope in his other hand. In his pocket there was his knife and some money tied up in a handkerchief. The words we had read together came back to my mind: "I dreamed and behold I saw a man clothed with rags, standing in a certain place, with his face from his own house, a book in his hand, and a great burden upon his back."

We stood at the end of our wagon trail and watched Bob as he turned to the north, walking on alone. The dog started to follow him, then she saw us remaining where we were, and she turned around, bewildered and undecided which direction she should take. We saw Bob reach the top of the hill, then he went down, out of sight, first his legs, then his shoulders and his head. I thought of our mornings at the creek when he jumped in the water, disappearing from view, with ripples rising up from where he was. There was not even a ripple now, nor a splash to show where he went.

I wrote my first book at that time, and called it *Robin on the Mountain*. It was a book for children, the kind of story Bob liked to hear at night before he went to sleep. It was not about him, but he came into it, as he came into many of the following books, in the little things he had done such as making tracks in the forest like a bear's, by walking on his hands, teaching tricks to a spotted dog, laboring over extracting tar from pine chips.

I read each chapter of the book to Vannie, as it was written. When I used a word or a phrase she did not understand, I explained it to her in a simpler form, and I used that phrase or word instead. The colloquial speech I heard all about me seemed natural to use, but I gave up trying to spell the words as they are pronounced in the mountain dialect. I used the normal spelling, as one does when writing the speech of a Bostonian or a New Yorker, though one may not put in his *r*'s and the other uses too many. There are fine shades of pronunciation that cannot be put down on paper. The mountaineer's "where" is something between "whar" and "whirr," but neither spelling can express it. And so it is with his other words.

Bob's abandoned wheelbarrow still lay on the ground beside the automobile, and we had to step over his bucket and pipe for making tar when we went out to the calf lot. At all hours of the day, there was something to remind us of him, and when we sat quietly sewing, with our thoughts far away, one of us would speak up, now and then, and say, "Wonder what Bob is doing now?" or "He must have found his sister's place all right. He couldn't very well have missed it."

He did not write to let us know. The wilderness had drawn its curtain over him as it had done to his sister and to Mrs. Lewis when she left her old homeplace. In a place where the art of storytelling has still survived, the art of letter writing has never begun.

Chapter XXI

GORDON HALE was shot for a wild turkey by one of the men on his place. He was hidden in the underbrush, making the turkey call when he was hunting in the woods, and the man aimed the gun in the direction of the noise, and fired. Now he was said to be dying, deserted by everyone except his nephew. Even the toothless woman had gone away, taking her child with her. The nephew had ridden his horse to a lather to fetch old Doctor Pearce, who was with him now, doing what he could. The news spread over the valley.

From the time when he first came to the valley to live, Gordon Hale had wanted nothing to do with his neighbors. He had gone his own way, and his way was no affair of ours, he let us know. There had been dark rumors reaching us from time to time of strange things going on at the place. It was not because he made whiskey. That in itself was not looked upon as a great wrong. But there were other things, mysterious hints dropped here and there, of one who came from no one knew where, and another who silently disappeared. It was told that Gordon Hale and his men set fire to every vacant house in the valley so no strangers would come in, but none could say for sure. We only knew that, soon after a family moved away, the house always burned down, and Daddy Means' house had burned when he was only out hunting.

Now the man was wounded and deserted, and if ever a one needed the help and friendship of his neighbors, Gordon Hale did. We talked it over among ourselves and in the end we decided to go to him. I think our minds were made up from the beginning, when we first heard the news. But it was Jock Wheeler who put our thoughts in words.

"I figure I wouldn't leave a yellow dog off by himself to die," he said. "And I couldn't do a man worse than I'd do a dog."

I hesitated about taking Vannie with me, but the Nixon girls went, and Lizzie Wells and the Widow Johnson took their children along. The men went first. Uncle George, who had a way with sick people, helped old Doctor Pearce take out the lead from the wounded man's shoulder.

At twilight I went to the Hale place with the women. We had to walk across the creek on a log, and I watched anxiously until I saw Lizzie Wells safely over, for her steps were heavy in her pregnancy. She balanced herself carefully, holding the last baby in her arms. The children waded, with trousers and skirts rolled up, splashing the water before them, and shouting at one another. We passed the place where I found the yellow cat, but there was no sign of a burned house now. The charred logs had become part of the earth and the grass grew over to hide them. Vines sprawled over the ground as if they had always grown that way. In spite of the friendly noises of the barnyard animals, there was a mysterious and deserted look about the place.

Gordon Hale was as pale as death and his eyes were sunk

in his head. He turned feebly toward us when we entered the room, but he did not speak. He lay on an old rumpled quilt thrown over the bed, and his pillow was dirty, with no case on it. I could see the eyes of Lizzie Wells, who could not abide untidiness, glance here and there about the unkept room, and I knew she was mentally sweeping and scrubbing and dusting to put it in order. But we did nothing that night more than bathe his head with cold water to take down the fever. We were there to show him that he was not friendless and alone. We did the same to all who were sick in the valley, and the same would be done for us.

I thought of clean hospital beds and skilled doctors and nurses, and drugs to ease a man's pain as I sat in the room with my neighbors. A bullet wound in the shoulder was not a serious thing, with the proper treatment. But the road was rough and long to the nearest hospital, and even in an automobile or truck his chance of surviving the trip was small. He was better off here in his own home, with those who lived near to come and sit with him and do what they could to make him comfortable.

Darkness came, and we lit the one lamp, first cleaning the accumulated soot on the chimney, and we put a piece of paper from a big match box on the side to keep the glare from the sick man's eyes. His side of the room was in shadow, and we sat in the concentrated glow in the other corner. The night was hot and noisy. Moths flew in to hover over the lamp and the insects kept up their steady song. We were more conscious than ever of the persistent call of the whippoorwill, for it was a sign of death when he flew near.

The men went out on the porch where it was cooler, and

we could hear the drone of their voices, with their words coming in now and then.

"Judge not, lest ye be judged," Jock Wheeler quoted his favorite passage from the *Bible*.

Then I heard Uncle George say, "A man talking in a fever's not always telling what's so. He can't be held for what he tells then."

Old Doctor Pearce came in from the porch and took some brown powder from his bag which he mixed in a glass of water to give the wounded man. Mrs. Wheeler helped raise his head until the medicine was down, then the doctor took the glass with a shudder.

"Bitterest tasting medicine in the world," he said. "Gags me just to give it."

In spite of modern hospitals and an excellent medical college in my state, there are isolated settlements such as ours, which must be reached by rough, winding roads impossible for automobiles to travel, where the only medical treatment to be had is from some old Granny woman with wisdom of long experience, or a hill farmer with a special aptitude for healing the sick. Doctor Pearce was such a man, and so was my grandfather, before him. In their youth, the state was more lenient in allowing a man to practice medicine. They had only to answer a few questions and they were given their license.

Old Doctor Pearce was one of the last of his kind. He lived far beyond the valley, alone, for his wife was dead, and when he was at home long enough, he cultivated a garden and raised a few fruit trees, which he loved to keep pruned and tended. He left the childbirths and the care of

little children to the old Granny women, such as Granny
Massery, who knew the cures of the herbs and roots, and
the ordinary remedies such as turpentine and lard and
quinine. He came in for the more serious illnesses. Though
he had read as many books as he could afford to buy, on dis-
eases and their cures, his knowledge had come to him
through instinct and experience, sitting at the bedside of
patients for three generations. There was something about
this tall, gaunt man with stooped shoulders and thin grey
hair that gave confidence to the sick. He stayed with them
during their illness, sleeping where there was room for him,
and leaving only when they were well, or when there was
someone else who needed him more. And his fee was whatever his patients felt they could afford.

None of his patients hated medicine more than Doctor
Pearce himself. He invariably made a face and turned his
head when a sick person swallowed the stuff he gave, and
he never recommended castor oil for that was too vile a dose
for mortal man, he declared.

He grieved doubly over the loss of a patient, for it was the
loss of a friend and neighbor, too, as he was known for
many miles around. But he had never lost a patient, he liked
to boast, except where the Lord saw fit to take him anyway.

The Lord would surely see fit to take Gordon Hale, we
thought as we sat in the room with him that night. The
man made no sound as he lay there, white against the dark
quilt and pillow in the shadowy corner. He was as still as
death except his twitching hands picking at the quilt he lay
upon. Then they were still. Mrs. Nixon tiptoed to the bed
and put her ear down to hear if his heart were still beating,
and she nodded that it was when she came back to us.

The children had grown sleepy and lay down on the floor. Several times in the night I thought I saw Bob there, as one of the Johnson boys or the Wells boy, in blue overalls and tousled hair, turned over to sleep on the other side. Mrs. Wheeler nodded her head and my eyes began to feel heavy. Now and then one of the men on the porch lit a match to his pipe and his face stood out of the darkness for an instant, showing lines caused by the wind and sun and the sweat of hard work, and it was lost again. They were only voices now, talking of death and ghosts, and wondering what it was like to be so close to the other side. The nephew of Gordon Hale sat with them, but he was silent and did not join in their conversation.

The old doctor went back to the kitchen where he made a pallet on the floor so he could get some sleep. At regular intervals, all during the night, he woke up to mix his powders to give the patient, and he never failed to make a face and shudder while it was going down.

"Gordon Hale, I've done all I can do for you, now," he said, just as dawn began to light the sky. "There's nothing more I can do but pray for you. You're likely to meet your Maker this very night."

He stood beside the bed and bowed his head and prayed aloud, and Jock Wheeler, who came silently into the room, murmured, "Thy will be done, O Lord."

When Gordon Hale took a turn for the better, we thought at the time, and I think it still, that it was the presence of the old man standing above him, and perhaps the presence, too, of his neighbors there, that gave him courage to fight death.

We left him when morning came, for we had our own work to do. But at twilight we returned to sit all night again with him. We brought clean sheets and pillow slips, and Lizzie Wells, when she could stand the filth and dirt no longer, began to sweep and scrub, moving her heavy body gracefully about the room. We helped her bring in ashes and sand to whiten the floors and table. Even Mag Massery pitched in and washed the dirty dishes that were piled on the kitchen table. Mrs. Wheeler and Granny Massery, the two oldest women, bathed the patient in lukewarm water and put clean clothes on him. In the evening we cooked his food, chicken broth and corn meal mush simmering slowly on the back of the stove, for the doctor and his nephew to give him during the day.

When Gordon Hale was well enough so that he did not need us any more, we went back to our own affairs, and left him alone with his.

Now the men talked among themselves so that their wives heard and repeated it to one another, that Gordon Hale in his delirium had confessed to killing two men in Kentucky where he had come from. He had not said a word about throwing the man in the creek, or burning empty houses in the valley. If he had confessed to that, something might have been done about it. But Kentucky was far away and it had happened long ago, and besides, the man had talked in a high fever, so we said nothing about it to anyone outside the valley.

Chapter XXII

THERE was talk of having a singing class in the schoolhouse on the hill, with hymns and prayers. The
preacher that had come every year to hold meetings had
gone away to another state and no one had offered to take
his place. A pie supper was planned to bring a singing
teacher from the county north of us.

I was tired from the long walks I had taken every evening
to sit up with Gordon Hale when he was sick, and the climb
up the steep hill every morning to do the chores in the heat
of midsummer. I knew that the pie supper, as all parties
held in the valley, would last the whole night, until dawn
came to light the way home. I thought of reasons why I
could not go. But Vannie must not miss it, I decided, for
she needed to be with young people more.

"I can't see a bit of harm in your going down in the broad
daylight, alone," I said.

After all, Bob, three years younger, had gone on to Yell
County alone with no one to show him the way. We passed
no one on the trail that led to the dirt highway. It was like
having a private driveway for almost three miles. And once
on the road, she had less than four miles to walk, to reach
Rufus Wells' place. Surely nothing could happen to the
girl between my place and his. The custom of forbidding a

young girl to go out in the woods alone dated back to the days when there were bears and panthers and wolves, when even a grown man needed the protection of his gun. But that reason had passed. Vannie was a little surprised at my suggestion.

"You could stop at the Wells' and go down the rest of the way in the wagon with them," I went on. "Would you be afraid to do that?"

"I'm not afraid of e'er a thing," she replied.

"Then you can go home with your folks from the pie supper, and come back in the next wagon passing this way," I said.

She pressed her white Swiss dress and polished her white shoes, and I baked a plum pie and made dainty sandwiches, which we put in a box. We wrapped it with tissue paper and tied it with a red ribbon saved from our Christmas parcels. Vannie had used the ribbon for her hair, and we pressed it for the occasion.

"I'll fold it up and bring it back when the supper is over," she said.

She put some Queen Anne's lace and chickweed in the bow to make it even prettier.

"I hope Daddy Means isn't the one to bid for this box," I teased.

We laughed at the thought of having him for a supper partner.

It was early in the afternoon when I saw Vannie start off, wearing her white lace-trimmed dress and carrying her clean white shoes in one hand and the box in the other. There would be time to reach the valley long before dark, I told my conscience, as I turned back to the house. It was a silly custom anyway, not to trust a girl in the woods alone. What harm could possibly come to her?

Daddy Means came riding by on his jenny soon after, and stopped to talk.

"Just saw Vannie down the way, walking by herself," he said.

I was a little annoyed, but I tried not to show it.

"Had she reached the road yet?" I asked.

"Near about. Is she going down all the way to the valley by herself?"

"Yes. She's on her way to the pie supper," I replied, with a strong desire to add that it was none of his business, anyway. Instead I turned the conversation. "What's the news from the valley?"

"The Widow Johnson got a letter today from her sister."

"Yes?"

"The sister's boy got killed in an automobile up in Springfield."

"Do you mean Alan?" I asked, anxiously.

"Yes—two other girls and a boy with him, and him supposed to be getting married to the Duncan girl back home. He was the only one killed. They're bringing his body home to be buried."

It was strange to think of Alan, so undecided all his life, doing a thing so definite as to die. A singing, laughing, teasing personality, going from one plan to another, and one girl to another, had now become a body, spoken of as *it* instead of *he*. There was no changing his mind now. What he had done at last, was done for good and all.

I thought suddenly of Vannie, dressed in her best clothes, on her way to the pie supper.

"Did you tell Vannie?" I asked.

"Yes," the old man answered.

His voice implied wonder that I should ask him that. News traveled that way. It was how we learned about things that were happening. We met and we passed the word along.

I was glad now that Vannie was on her way to the pie supper, in her best dress, with a daintily wrapped box. And I hoped Bill Wells, or some handsome boy who could sing and laugh, would buy it and eat with her.

The Widow Johnson came up the Rocky Crossing road the next morning, on her way to her sister's home, but only her six sons were with her. I asked about Vannie, and she replied that she had not seen her.

"She went down to the pie supper," I said. "She promised to come back when the next wagon came this way."

"She wasn't at her folks' this morning. They said nothing about her coming there at all," Mrs. Johnson answered.

The two older boys went to the well to draw water for the mules, but Mrs. Johnson was in a hurry to get to her sister's before the funeral, and she did not come in.

"Vannie was going to stop at the Wells' and go to the pie supper with them," I said.

I was very much alarmed now.

"The Wells said nothing about her, either, and I don't think she was at the pie supper, for I heard nothing about it. Of course, though, I and my boys didn't go there."

My plea of being too tired to go down to the valley the night before resulted in much weary walking there, asking everyone I knew about Vannie. No one had seen her, or had even heard from her. Mag and Jeff came out of their apathy enough to express concern. Jeff even considered hitching up his wagon and going off in search of her.

"She probably went to the funeral," I said. "Daddy Means told her of Alan's death when she was on her way to the valley."

"Then in reason she'll be coming back with the Widow Johnson," Jeff said. "I'd likely miss her if I went out after her now."

I had expected sympathy from Granny, who had lived her own life as she chose, but she was less tolerant than the others.

"She had no call to go traipsing off by herself like that," she remarked.

"It wasn't her fault," I said. "I let her go, for I didn't want her to miss the fun just because I didn't feel up to the long walk."

"She ought to know better anyway," Granny went on. "But she always was mulish."

"She did know better," I insisted. "But she knew if she refused to come down alone, I would come with her rather than let her miss the party. She did it to spare me."

"Well, why didn't she come then, like she said she would?" Granny wanted to know.

I could not answer. Rumors began to come in at last, brought by one and another passing through the valley. A young girl was seen running along the Cherry Hill road in her bare feet, carrying her shoes in her hand, on the day of the pie supper. Someone else had seen a young girl dressed in white, in an automobile parked at a deserted place, on the Cherry Hill road, with five men in it, passing a jar of whiskey from one to the other. Other tales followed.

"She took it hard about the boy's death," Rufus Wells said.

"The kind that takes it hard like that is the kind that gets over it soon," Lizzie put in.

Lizzie decided to go home with me, and Rufus hitched the wagon to drive us up the hill.

"It's best if we stay here and wait for her, so there'll be somebody here when she comes," Lizzie said.

It was comforting to be with Lizzie. She brought her two youngest children with her, and the time would soon come for the next one. The little girl talked constantly, to make up for her mother's silence. She lived in a world of make-believe. Sometimes she was a grown lady, looking after a family of children made of sticks, washing their clothes and putting them to bed, and sometimes she was a rabbit, hopping about the room. She and her small brother sat on kitchen chairs and took a trip to town in a make-believe wagon drawn by make-believe mules, to look for Vannie.

"She's coming now," the child said, and I paid no attention, for I thought it was still her play.

"I vow, the young one is right," Lizzie said, looking out the open door.

I saw Vannie turn in at the gate and walk slowly down the path as if she were not sure whether she could come in or not. Her dress was rumpled and stained with dirt, and the lace was torn, hanging down and dragging as she walked. Her hair was matted and there was a bruise over her left eye. She carried only one white shoe in her hand, with no explanation where the other was.

My first impulse was to cry out, "Where on earth have

you been?" But I checked myself. Lizzie's presence there had taught me to keep silent.

Whatever the girl had done, I knew that everything depended on how she was received now. She would become sullen and stubborn if I began to question her, or tried to preach a sermon to her. She would justify herself in her mind and say it was not wrong. Besides, had I not committed the first wrong by letting her start out in the woods alone? I had gone over these things in my mind so many times as I waited in silence with Lizzie Wells. I forced a calmness upon myself which I did not feel.

"Come in, Vannie," I said, opening the screen door for her.

Lizzie quietly heated some water in the kettle and took it to the washroom.

"You look tired," she said to the girl. "Don't you want to bathe and change your clothes and lie down to rest?"

While she was in the washroom I took off her couch cover and prepared the bed, though it was only a little after noon. She went in quietly to her room and slept the clock around. It was good for her and for us, for we could talk together more naturally when she got up, after her long rest, and came into the kitchen with us to drink a bowl of soup and a glass of hot milk.

The Widow Johnson returned and came in to sit with me, and to bring me the news from the county seat. She told of the funeral, and of the people there.

"But I saw nothing of Vannie," she said.

"No, Vannie is here," I replied, without telling her when or how she had arrived.

I knew she would spread word in the valley of the girl's return. We would stay on the hill until the news was old, and Vannie would not be met with questions and embarrassed silences. Lizzie went back with her in the wagon, and I knew that Vannie's secret would be kept.

It did not take Vannie long to recover from the battered, bruised girl that had turned in at the gate, hesitating and afraid to come in. We went about our daily routine as we had always done, and we sat for lessons in the rose garden, late in the afternoon. She read about Rima from *Green Mansions,* stumbling over the words she did not understand. Once, when the rooster jumped awkwardly up in the air to catch a grasshopper, she laughed aloud, then she stopped suddenly, as if she had done wrong to laugh.

Again I heard her in the washroom, splashing water for her sponge bath, singing, "It's raining, it's pouring——"

The words stopped suddenly and there was silence. Then there came, "Amazing grace, how sweet the sound."

Later the empty fruit jar disappeared from her bureau drawer and took its place with the other jars on the pantry shelf. She became her old self again. She began to talk and laugh and sing as naturally as she had done when she first came to me, though her eyes had lost their old shyness, that look of a young fawn. Instead I saw something I had seen in the eyes of her grandmother, something old and wise.

At the creek, in the shade of the button willows, where the water lilies with their yellow blossoms grew in a clustered mass, I spoke to her.

"Did you go to his grave?" I asked.

"Yes."

"How did you get there?"

"I walked."

She said no more and I did not ask more. I took the advice Lizzie Wells had whispered to me when she left to go down with the Widow Johnson, "Best not plague her with questions. Best let her get over it."

I had already seen how legends grow, with a little more added at each telling. A girl seen running barefoot along the Cherry Hill road, with her shoes in her hand, a girl in an automobile drinking raw whiskey with five men, a girl taken off in the woods and raped five times. It was as easy now to believe the tale she told, that she had walked the thirty-five miles to the county seat to stand at Alan's grave, then walked thirty-five miles back home again. Now she had become as one suddenly released from some bondage.

Chapter XXIII

THE farmer has a hard master, one he dares not strike against. He cannot bargain for better harvests and shorter harvesting hours, nor for rain and sun at the time he needs it. He must take what he is given and make the best of it through drouth and flood and killing frost, and through insects and disease. Only those who can work on, accepting these things, are the successful ones. The rebels are the failures.

Jeff Massery had always envied the lot of the laborer. Rumors now came into the valley of mines and factories opening again with higher wages paid, and of public works where a man could earn more in a month digging ditches than he could in a year on a little hill farm. Now and then an automobile came by and stopped at Uncle George's store, and men in town clothes, with money in their pockets, got out to buy something. One was a coal miner from the northern part of the state, one worked in a lumber mill and one in a canning factory, two counties away. It was their talk that caused Jeff to make the move at last he had been talking about for so long, and leave his farm and growing crop, to try his luck elsewhere.

He drove to Rocky Crossing in his wagon with his family and his pitifully few household belongings, on his way to

Coal Hill, where workers were needed for the mines that were opening again. They spent the night with us to get an early start in the morning.

"I've not made up my mind whether I'm going on or not," Granny said at the supper table. "I've a good notion to stay on right here till you get up there and make up your mind whether you aim to stay on or not."

"What do you aim to do, Vannie? Reckon you'd want to go, too?" Mag asked.

"I've not made up my mind either," Vannie answered, and she turned to me, waiting for me to speak.

Mag looked at me, too, and I thought I saw a wistful look in her eyes. It was not easy, even for Mag, to give up her daughter without knowing when she would ever see her again. I wished they had not left the matter to me. Vannie had come of her own accord. The decision to stay should be her own, too. Since it was left to me, I could not decide against the girl's mother, for she was Mag's daughter and not mine, after all. Yet I did not want Vannie to feel my home was no longer hers.

"It might be a nice change for you to get out and meet new people," I said to Vannie. "Why don't you go with your folks and stay till they are settled in their new home, and then come back."

Little Ona put her head down close to her plate, as Vannie had done on that first day she came to me, and gulped her blackberry cobbler.

"Big sister, are you coming, too?" she asked.

"I reckon," Vannie replied.

"Are you going to sleep with me?"

"Yes."

I gave Vannie an old suitcase and helped her pack her clothes. She wanted to take only a few things, and leave the rest to come back to, but I knew she would need them all. It would be a long journey, going by wagon with only one sorry mule to pull it. There would be many stops overnight, camping in the open, along the way.

"They say a man scarce has to turn his hand to earn a day's wage there." Jeff was full of talk about the place where he was going.

I expected him to come back to his farm soon after he learned that the work was hard where he was going, as work is hard everywhere. When I said good-bye, it was with the feeling that I would see them all again. Granny hesitated, then she went out to the wagon, too, and climbed up on the wheel to get in with a spry step. I waved when they reached the bend in the road, then I turned back to a lonesome house.

"Jeff'll be back," Rufus Wells put my thoughts into words when I went to the valley next. "A fellow that goes off looking for easy work never finds it. A farmer thinks he'll find it easier in town where he can earn a regular wage, and a town man's always aiming to buy himself a little farm where he can take life easy. And wherever they go they find just what they've been running away from, hard work and plenty of it."

Rufus Wells, whose large, blunt hands were always busy, had never run away from hard work. His blacksmith shop and the house on the hill where Lizzie always welcomed me, was the first place I passed on my way to the valley. It was here that I learned the news of all that happened since I came down last. Bill had gone off, walking all the way to a college in the northern part of the state, where he could work for his board and education. They told me of his leaving.

"And Mrs. Lewis and her boy came this morning. They're spending the day with the Nixons," Lizzie said.

"You mean the one who had the homestead next to mine?" I asked.

She nodded. "First time in a right smart while she's been here."

Of course I knew that many years had passed, and her son could not possibly be the little towheaded boy in jeans, peeping shyly from his mother's skirts, as I had pictured him on my walks to their old homeplace. But I was not prepared for the fat, smug man I saw in Uncle George's store, complaining about the dirt road he had driven over.

"Hasn't changed since I was a boy," he said. "Why, I had to take my car right down in the river to cross, not even a wooden bridge over it. What do you do here when the water's up?"

"We don't cross it then," Uncle George replied.

I went to the back room where the women were, and I met at last my ghost neighbor in the flesh. She was about Mrs. Nixon's age, but her wrinkled face was covered with powder, with a daub of rouge on each cheek. Her hair was bobbed and tightly curled in a cheap permanent. She wore a sleazy rayon dress which the younger Nixon girl eyed enviously.

"I've gone to your homestead often," I said. "My flower garden is planted with your roses and narcissuses, and I have some of your lilacs and burning bushes, too."

"Good gracious, are those things still alive?" she asked, laughing.

Mrs. Nixon saw her daughters looking at the woman's curly short hair with admiring eyes.

"I declare you must have had a bad fever to make your hair fall out and come back so curly," she remarked.

"Oh, Mamma, that's a permanent wave," the oldest Nixon girl said, embarrassed for her mother.

Mrs. Nixon looked at me and winked, and I knew she was having her little joke. And I knew that Mrs. Lewis, sitting in the room with us, was farther away than she had ever been when she was in some place unknown to us. I thought of Vannie and Bob. I wondered what they would be like if they did return. Perhaps it was better when the wilderness draws its curtains over the ones who leave. They come back to us as strangers. Left in our memories, they stay as they were when we knew them well.

My mention of her flowers started Mrs. Lewis talking about the old days. She was bitter about them, for they had been hard.

"One time we took a trip in our wagon to town to buy what we had to have," she said. "My boy stood looking at a bunch of bananas in the store so long and so pitiful like, and he said, 'Mamma, does bananas cost money?' 'Yes, son, they cost money I've not got,' I had to say to him. And I've not forgot it to this day."

I caught a glimpse of the real woman then, but she was soon lost again as she began to boast of her home in Little Rock with electricity and running water, hot and cold. She had gone to the city after her husband's death, to give her children a chance to get on in the world. Perhaps it was the remark of her son, "Does bananas cost money?" that gave her the determination to give them the things they wanted, by keeping boarders and sewing for other people, until they were old enough to make their own way. Her son now could buy all the bananas he wanted, but she would always be haunted by the wistful question of the small boy he used to be.

Lizzie came out to the gate to greet me when I passed her on my way home. She and Rufus had harvested their crops early, so she would have nothing to do but care for the new baby when the time came. The sorghum and corn were stacked in the shed, the potato house was filled, and the cotton was piled high in the wagon, ready to be taken to the gin and sold.

"Wish you'd come in and spend the night with us," Lizzie said.

I thought of the long climb up the hill, with my ears straining through the silence for the familiar sounds of Vannie's singing and Bob's shouts as he played with his colt and the dog, and I accepted.

We sat on the porch after supper, with a cool breeze blowing through the open gallery. Rufus planed some lumber to make a small chest for the clothes Lizzie had made, and she and I hemmed bird's-eye cloth for diapers. The three young Wells children were playing in the wagon, rolling and tumbling in the soft bed of cotton. I wished it could always be this way, sitting in silent intimacy with those I was fond of, listening to the peaceful sounds of the barnyard animals settling down for the night, and the laughter of the children at play. We spoke very little, for we had no need for words. The light grew dim, and the children came in, tired and ready for bed.

"Think I'll take that cotton on to town while you're here," Rufus spoke up. "I don't like the notion of leaving Lizzie by herself the way she is."

"I want to go too, Papa. Can't I go too?" the boy called from the kitchen where he was washing his feet for bed. He came out on the porch to continue his plea.

"I'll look after your stock tomorrow on my way and I'll stop by Daddy Means and tell him to tend them while you're here," Rufus went on.

"Can't I go too, Papa?" his son said.

"I reckon. Now go on and get some sleep so you can get up early for we're bound to start before day."

Lizzie made a list of things she wanted him to buy with the cotton money. We measured the children's feet for new shoes, which excited them so that sleep was impossible for a while. I made a list, too, and I wrote out a check for him to cash for me.

"We'll pick peas at the Widow Johnson's while he's away," Lizzie said.

The year's cycle had come back, from harvest time to harvest time. Once more we watched the mules tread the circle to grind molasses from the sorghum cane, once more the cotton wagons slowly rolled on their way to the gin, dropping white fluffs along the roadside, and once more we were picking peas in the Widow Johnson's fields. I picked without complaint this time. It had been a good summer, and there was enough in my pantry for the coming winter, and for some lean year ahead. But I would always be haunted, as Mrs. Lewis was, by two hungry children sitting down to a dinner of corn meal mush and canned blackberries, and of barnyard animals calling out for the scraps that we left.

I was alone with Lizzie when her time came. Rufus had been gone for five days and we were expecting his return at any time. We had planned, that if he had not come back, I was to go, when she felt the first pain, and bring back Mrs. Wheeler, who had taken Granny's place in the valley. Ben could take word to Mrs. Nixon and the Widow Johnson.

But it happened too suddenly for me to leave her. I was sleeping across the gallery with the little girl, when I was awakened by Lizzie's call. I quickly dressed and lit the lamp to go to her, and I saw that I had no time to go to the Wheeler home.

I took the youngest child from her bed and carried him across the gallery, to sleep beside his sister. He stirred and began to cry, and I gently shook the bed until he dozed off again. If only the girl were a little older, I thought, to stay with her mother while I went out for help. I built a fire in the kitchen stove for the night was chilly, and I thought of what Granny Massery had told me she did to ease the pains of a woman in childbirth. She made a tea with the roots of black haw and bark from the north side of a red oak. I could do nothing like that for Lizzie Wells then. All I could do was to sit at her bedside and give her my hands to clasp tightly in hers, when she needed me. She told me later that it was an easy childbirth, but I suffered mentally with her as I watched her face in the lamplight and heard her low groans.

I heard someone approach on horseback.

"Will you be all right, Lizzie, while I run out and stop him, whoever it is?" I asked.

It was the dark of the moon and the night was like a curtain before me. In the starlight I groped for my step. The rise and fall of the earth which I did not notice during the day, loomed large before me now. A star fell, leaving a brilliant trail behind it. Vannie would say a soul was dying and going to heaven. I called out to the rider, and I saw a dim shadow of a horse come to a stop.

"Hello," I called, and Gordon Hale's voice answered.

I hesitated.

"Are you needing anything?" he asked.

"Lizzie Wells is having her baby," was all that I could think of then to say.

The man dismounted and hitched his horse to the gatepost, and followed me up the hill. In the light of the lamp I could see his thin, white face. He paused at the door, and I said, "I wanted to get word to Mrs. Wheeler."

"We've scarce time for that, I reckon," he replied, and he came in the room with me.

He knew no more than I did about babies, and we acted through instinct only, an instinct as old as the world. A string was needed, and I searched until I found strong quilting thread, which we used to tie the cord. Gordon took out his sharp knife and lifted the lamp chimney to sterilize it in the flame, and cut the cord. My mind ran from Granny's lore to the things I had been told of babies born in modern hospitals. They should be rubbed with olive oil, I had heard. But this baby was sponged in lukewarm water poured in a galvanized wash tub and put in a basket where a clean flour sack was spread over a folded quilt.

We had little to say to each other. I was like an automaton that night, going from Lizzie to the baby and back to Lizzie again. It was long after, when the picture came back to my mind, that I remembered the look in his face, still pale and drawn from his recent illness, as he held the crying baby tenderly in his two hands, and said to Lizzie Wells, "You've a little girl."

Perhaps, if the things he had confessed in his delirium were true, he was thinking that he had, in some way, compensated by helping to bring a new life into the world.

When the baby was in its basket and Lizzie was made comfortable, he went off to his waiting horse and rode away, back to his own life and we turned back to ours. But a tie had been formed that was to draw us together whenever he needed us and when we needed him.

Soon after he had gone, Mrs. Wheeler came, then Mrs. Nixon and the Widow Johnson, scolding because they had not been told sooner. They busied themselves putting the place back in order, and preparing breakfast, and making a fuss over the new baby.

"Have you decided what to name her?" I asked.

"No, I've not given it much thought," Lizzie answered. "Have you got any ideas?"

"Let's call her Vannie," I said.

Lizzie smiled as if she knew that was what it would be.

Chapter XXIV

I HAD two little notes from Vannie after she left, scrawled with pencil on lined tablet paper. In the first one she said that Granny had died. She wanted to come back home as soon as the folks didn't need her any more. Several months later the other letter came from the northern part of the state, where Jeff had gone, no doubt still searching for an easier life. She told me that she was going to be married soon to a farmer from Missouri. My answers to both letters came back marked "Address Unknown." Bob did not write at all but I received a package by mail addressed in his handwriting, containing an embroidered sofa pillow, the kind tourists buy when they go to Hot Springs. I knew that he had gone there and that he had thought of me.

When three years had passed and the bet with the government was won, with the title to the land mine at last, I left Rocky Crossing. Like Bob and Vannie, I expected to return soon, and I did not lock the doors. It was six years before I saw it after that. I lived in many places, in Kansas City, Santa Fé, in old Mexico, and that lonesomest of all cities, New York. It was there, in a hotel bedroom, one Christmas, that I received a coconut cake from Lizzie Wells, with MERRY XMAS written on it with raisins. It was surrounded by holly and mistletoe from Rocky Crossing. That alone made my Christmas a merry one.

When I felt homesick in hotel rooms and rented apartments, it was for my log house at Rocky Crossing. That was an anchor for me, a place where I could always go back and feel at home. And it stood there, waiting for me, as long as it could serve that purpose. It was when I turned away from it, even in my mind, that I lost it.

When John and I married, we planned to go back to Arkansas, which was his native state, also, and build a home together. We bought some land close to Little Rock and close to new friends we had grown fond of. We chose a site overlooking the Arkansas River, deep in the pine woods. The house was to be made of native stone, and the architect drew the plans.

"Let's live at Rocky Crossing while the house is being built," I said.

There was a new road leading to Rocky Crossing, with concrete bridges over rivers and streams that we used to cross on logs, or by wading. The road skirted the valley to take a straighter course, and there was a new store and filling station kept by a stranger from the city. I could see the old road leading through the valley, untraveled now except by occasional wagons of those who lived there. I thought of Mrs. Lewis who came back after many years, and I would not go that way then. I would wait until I was living at Rocky Crossing again, in the way I had once lived there. I would not be a stranger to them then. We could go back beyond the six years that had passed, and visit with each other in the same intimacy we once knew.

There were signs of campers having used my house.

Notices of hunting laws were left by hunters. Fishermen from the city and lumberjacks who came to cut the timber, had walked in and made themselves at home. On the floor of the kitchen I saw an old patchwork quilt, a tin cup and plate, and some food which a recent camper had left.

A carpenter from Little Rock was sent to mend the sagging doors and replace the broken windowpanes, and to put in a kitchen sink and plumbing in the washroom. I went out again when it was finished, and took a woman with me to get the place in order. We scrubbed the floors and stained them and we put up new curtains and new cushions for the chairs. Except for the plumbing and the refrigerator and new white range in the kitchen, the place was like it had been when I lived there. It was so lovely to me, that even after I had locked the door that evening, I turned back and opened it again to have one more look at the soft pine color of the walls and ceilings, and the wide fireplaces, clean now and ready for logs, and the crisp cotton curtains at the windows. In three days from then, we planned to move there and live the whole summer while the new house was going up. In three more days, once more in my old home, and no longer a stranger who had gone away to live in the city, I could see the Wells and the Nixons and the Wheelers and the Widow Johnson again.

On the night before we were to move, there was a terrific thunderstorm. We could see the lightning flash through the north window of the hotel room, and the thunder roared over the noise of the traffic. People on the street below hurried over the wet pavement with their umbrellas held before them, to get out of the storm. I thought of the electric storms I had seen at Rocky Crossing, with tall pines catching the bolts all around me. It had been like living on a battlefield, with bombs bursting on all sides, but there was a beauty about it I did not find in city storms.

By morning the storm clouds had gone. The sun came out, and the day was mild and warm. A moving van went ahead of us, with some furniture I wanted to keep at Rocky Crossing. When we came to the new store, on the highway skirting the valley, we saw the moving van waiting for us. I stopped the car and the man who owned the store came up to speak to us.

"I've bad news for you," he said. "Can you take it, whatever it is?"

"My house—" I began.

"Burned to the ground, last night, in the storm."

I tried to grasp his words as he spoke, but my mind went back to other houses there that had burned.

"Gordon Hale," I said. "There's a man here named Gordon Hale."

"Gordon Hale's been dead for a couple of years," the man said, and his voice was gentle as if he were trying to humor a person talking in delirium. He went on, repeating what he had evidently been saying, "Struck by lightning, the forest ranger saw it at the tower. Rufus Wells and I went up there this morning with him to look at it, and it had been struck all right. There's no doubt about that."

The moving van went back to Little Rock to store our furniture in the warehouse, but I wanted to go on to Rocky Crossing. We saw only the two tall chimneys, with ashes still smouldering between them. It was like standing beside a grave, searching for some loved one and finding only the earth and a stone. The heavy cedar logs that were the bottom logs were not burned through, but there was nothing left of the large ridge pole that was the first to catch fire.

It was two years before I could bring myself to go there again, to spread a picnic lunch on the ground between the two chimneys, and look out at the mountains in the distance, watching them change colors with the sun. I had come again to look upon Rocky Crossing, not as a place that was dead, but a place to be built again.

Chapter XXV

I TURNED to the boy who sat on a rock beside us. His
dog had scented the rabbit and had left him to give
chase.

"You are Virgil Johnson," I said.

He looked up and smiled.

"Yes, and I bet I know who you are, now. I could see it
when I talked about your house burning."

I tried to see the chubby little cheeks smeared with icing
from the birthday cake, and the mischievous eyes smiling at
me, but I could not. I could only see his older brother's face
now, the top one of the stair steps of boys. I asked about
them, and he said that the three oldest had gone off to war.
Another one, nearly eighteen, would be going soon.

"Has Bill Wells gone, too?" I asked.

"Yes, him and his brother. And Ben Wheeler and Bob
Jenkins, too. In five more years, I'll be eighteen, and I
can go."

"Bob Jenkins?" I repeated.

"Yes. Ben Wheeler wrote his folks he was there in the
Solomon Islands where Ben is. They're there together."

"Did he come back, then?" I asked.

"Yes, when he got old enough to live where he wanted to,

he came back. Stayed with us a while, but he used to come up here and camp a lot, by himself."

Bob Jenkins was back at Rocky Crossing alone, and now in the Solomon Islands. We had never got around to studying about the Solomon Islands in our lessons. His words came back to me.

"Tell me about a Chinaman."

I had put him off by saying, "One thing at a time, Bob. We'll talk about that side of the world when we are through with Europe."

Now Bob would have things to tell me about that side of the world.

Was he fighting for Rocky Crossing and the valley, I wondered. It was the only home he had ever known except the orphanage that he had rebelled against. I had seen for myself, later, how well the orphanages of Little Rock were run. Bob had been treated well there, but he had been too free to endure even the little regimentation any boy must have, in growing up. There would be no regimenting Bob now that he was grown. He would fight to the bitter end against that.

"Did you ever hear anything about Vannie?" I asked, feeling like a Rip van Winkle come back after a long sleep.

He thought I meant Vannie Wells, but I shook my head.

"Vannie Massery," I said.

He had never heard of her, though he remembered the old Massery homeplace in the valley.

If Bob came back, it was possible to believe that she might come some day, too, and bring her family. I wondered if she told them about Rocky Crossing as it used to be, when we were there together.

"I'm going to build it back again, just as it was," I said.
There are still tall pines standing in the forest to make
the walls and roof, and rocks for the foundation.

When Bill Wells and Bob and Ben come back, we'll have
another house here just like the old one.

"Retreat to the Land"

O VER *a decade before her memoir* Straw in the Sun *was published, Charlie May Simon wrote of her homesteading experience and the lives of the self-reliant hill people in "Retreat to the Land," an article that appeared in* Scribner's Magazine *in May 1933. In sharp contrast to Simon's apparent solitary venture in the memoir, the presence of her husband, Howard, in the* Scribner's *piece reveals their joint effort, whereas in her memoir he is a "ghost," mentioned only by the boy in the opening and closing chapters: "they," not "she," is the pronoun he uses to refer to the people who had lived in the cabin, now destroyed by fire. Beyond the striking reality of Howard's presence, the magazine article differs significantly in tone from the writer's voice Simon adopts in her memoir. While the article reflects an outsider's commentary on the customs and superstitions of the Ozark hill people, the memoir reveals Simon as an accepted member of the community. Interestingly, Howard Simon also wrote of the homesteading experience, almost thirty years after the publication of* Straw in the Sun. *In his memoir, he is alone: Charlie May and the children are excluded in the selected memories he presents in* Cabin on a Ridge.*

Publishing "Retreat to the Land," reproduced here, accomplished three things for the author: it provided money for food during her last year of homesteading; generated public attention that created the link with her future publisher, E. P. Dutton; and introduced John Gould Fletcher and Vance Randolph to her writing. When the Simons left Arkansas for New York City in the summer of 1935, after completing the three years required for establishing a homestead claim, Charlie May grew discontented with city life, missing Possum Trot (identified as Rocky Crossing in the memoir). She returned to Arkansas, later married John Gould Fletcher, and remained a resident of Little Rock until her death on March 21, 1977.

Retreat to the Land
An Experience in Poverty
CHARLIE MAY SIMON

A GROUP of us were having tea one Sunday afternoon at our studio in New York. As may be expected, we were discussing the depression. There were, besides Howard, who is an artist, and myself, a stock broker, a publisher, a writer, and a dancer. We did not know the first thing about economics, but we freely expressed our opinions and theories.

As I listened to them my thoughts turned to a cabin of our own in some wilderness, with a garden patch, a pig, a cow, and some chickens, and perhaps even a sheep and a loom, for we were in a receptive mood then. When I glanced at Howard I saw an expression in his face that reminded me of the time six years ago, in the Latin Quarter of Paris, when he asked me to marry him four days after we met. When our company had gone I was not surprised when he said to me, "Will you go?" and I answered, "Of course."

Howard counted up the month's bills. He found that we had exactly eight hundred and fifty-seven dollars and some cents after they were paid, including the return deposit of the electric company. We were interested in the same things, and were not bored with each other. Of course our venture would succeed. We did not mind giving up luxuries, those toys of civilization that had been invented in the last generation or so. All we asked of life was a little food, shelter, clothes enough for warmth, and peace and leisure to do the things we wanted to do.

So one morning, a few weeks later, we got into our Ford roadster and started west. We settled in the Ozark Mountains of Arkansas, following the footsteps of a long-ago ancestor. We were not long in filing a homestead claim on sixty acres of virgin pine forest, and started in on the job of wresting a living from the soil. Here we have been for over a year and a half.

We are thirty miles from the nearest railroad, telephone, or radio. A dirt road winds its way through our wilderness, but the creeks are unbridged and have to be forded when swollen by winter rains. Sometimes they are impassable, and our mail is held up when the mail carrier who brings it from the railroad to our little postoffice [sic] cannot cross on his mule. Rumors reach us by the grapevine system, and they are even more garbled than newspaper reports.

"They say Mr. Hoover's started a war on Chiny, or somewhere," we were told during the Japanese invasion of Manchuria. And just before the election Uncle Bill Taylor said that Doctor Evans said that some one told him if the Republicans got in, every man, woman and child would receive a hundred dollars. But there was no talk of depression, and here, we decided, was the ideal place to build our home.

Our nearest neighbor for five miles on one side is old Uncle John, who lives alone with two half-starved hound dogs in a tumbledown shack. He cooks over the fireplace and sleeps on what appears to be a bundle of rags, though they were at one time patchwork quilts. He hid from us for several weeks, and we learned that it was because his trousers were too torn to be patched any more. But his modesty gradually left him, and he often comes to sit and chat, always saying as he leaves, as though he was just about to forget it, "By the way, kin I borry a little_____?"

On the other side, our nearest neighbor is six miles away, a tall and gawky young man, Oval, and his equally tall and gawky wife, Ameriky. A short time after we arrived here, they came calling in a home-made vehicle with no two wheels alike, drawn by a pair of lean mules. Ameriky brought her two weeks' old baby.

"I just been duncey to see yore place," she told me. "But the little one here war borned on the day youens come. Hits name's Jewel."

Oval, dressed in the conventional overalls and a little straw hat that covered less than half of his shocky blonde hair, had nothing to say at first. He sat smoking one cigarette after another, rolling them in strips of catalog paper with home-grown tobacco, and striking the matches on the bare soles of his feet. Finally he asked Howard to step outside.

"I jist wanted to say," he said, "that when I hearn youens war a livin' here, I lowed there war a goin' to be trouble. But

I see youens know how to mind yore business, and I wan ter shake hands with you and say I'm yore friend." With that he reached back in his overall pocket and drew out a quart fruit jar filled with white corn whiskey, and shoved it out toward Howard.

The log house, with its huge stone fireplaces, slowly grew to look like the drawings Howard had made in New York. It is just large enough to meet the needs of two people: a studio, a library, a kitchen, a bedroom and a washroom, with plumbing, such as it is, by an expert moonshiner. The rooms are built around a stone-paved courtyard bordered with wild flowers transplanted from the woods. We had labor at fifty cents and a dollar a day, depending on the size of the family of the workers. They taught us many things about making a house without the use of boughten things, how to rive shingles from a board tree, and how to make the large wooden hinges and latches for the doors. With Howard's help they made most of the furniture. Howard carved the oak doors with pictures of the wild animals about us and painted murals on the walls. I was kept busy making cushions and curtains of gingham and hooking rag rugs.

If we were uncomfortable while this was going on, we did not know it. It was not until the house was finished and screened in that we thought of the flies swarming through the unchinked walls, and the yellowjackets that drove us away from the table whenever we had wild honey for breakfast, the nightly delousing of chiggers and ticks that crawled onto us from the bushes, and the noises of the screech owls, foxes, wildcats, wolves, and even one night the unearthly scream of a panther.

We planted our garden without knowing it first had to be fertilized, and nothing came up. So we brought sacks of fertilizer from the cow lot of an abandoned homestead, and spread it over the garden, and planted again. Every morning as soon as we got out of bed, we went out into our garden and watched it grow, from the baby seedlings on, counting each new leaf that formed. We hoed out every little weed that stuck up its head, and when the sun beat down too hot and strong, we drew bucket after bucket of water and carried it to the garden. It grew, a little puny, perhaps, for it was on new ground, but it pleased us. And then came a herd of wild cattle and ate every thing down in one night. We ran out in our night clothes and beat on a tin dish pan to frighten them, but as soon as we went into the house again, they came back, and we had to go to sleep to the sound of the crunching of our corn and beans. With the help of a young mountain boy we made a fence of palings, and planted again, with no thought of heroism, but with the determination that our venture should not fail.

"Youens hadn't ort to plant yore beans on flower-pot day," said the boy, "caze they'll all turn to blossom and won't make beans."

So because he seemed to know, and because he had a successful garden, we waited until twin days to plant the beans and peas, and the corn was planted in the dark of the moon and the potatoes were planted in the light of the moon, and the watermelons at midnight on the first of the month. Whether it was the fence or the fertilizer or the phase of the moon, our garden grew, and supplies us with food.

We bought a cow and her calf and some chickens. The cow is allowed to roam the mountains and feed herself on mountain grass, coming back each night and morning to be milked. The chickens feed themselves on grass and grasshoppers and what cornbread and buttermilk we have left. Inefficient perhaps, but we have enough milk and eggs for our needs. We trade for what food we do not grow. The mountain people are fond of trading, as money is scarce here. A shirt of Howard's brought a bushel of black-eyed peas, and a dress of mine brought two gallons of sorghum molasses and a peck of corn meal. The woods are full of wild berries and grapes, and if we cared for hunting and fishing, there are all around us deer, wild turkey, quail, rabbits and squirrels, and the creeks are full of bass and trout.

Savannah, a husky mountain girl of fourteen, came to us one morning and asked if she might work for us in exchange for her clothes and an education.

"Pappy caint buy me shoes to wear to school," she said, "and I want to larn books."

The soles of her shoes were tied on with strings, and her dress of many patches was of a nondescript color. This was all she had, and it was worn out in the fields to pick cotton, at night to sleep in, and on Saturdays she washed it and wore it on Sundays when her beau came a talking.

I realized how little one can learn in a two-months-a-year-backwoods country school when during her geography lesson I once asked her if she knew what shape the earth was.

"I don't know," she replied, "I've hearn some say hits round and some says hits squar."

And when I gave her the fairy tales to read that I thought every child was familiar with, she could not understand them because she had no idea what a king or queen or a fairy was. She is a bright child and eager to learn. It was not long before she had quit sassering her coffee and knifing her peas. Giving up her snuff was the hardest thing for her to do, for she loved to sit at one end of the room and spit between her teeth into the fireplace on the other end, and she was proud of her accuracy.

Every morning she washes, irons, or scrubs, and draws the water and keeps the fires going, and every afternoon she bathes and changes her clothes and I hear her lessons. I traded an etching to a New York friend for two pairs of shoes and some dresses, and a friend from Chicago sent her some sweaters and handkerchiefs and underwear in exchange for a wood engraving. Now Savannah is well clothed, and she knows that the earth is round and that Columbus discovered America, and she has a faint idea that a king is a boss of a whole lot of people and land.

After the house was finished and the garden growing, and Savannah was well established in the household, we had about two hundred and fifty dollars of the money we brought with us. By this time we had given away, traded or worn out nearly all of our clothes, and we decided to buy substantial woollen and khaki clothes that would last a long time. Too, we had more leisure and we could subscribe to some magazines and books by the month. We sent off checks for the magazines and books, and we went in to Little Rock for one more fling, a movie, dinner at a hotel, and shopping. A few days after, we received word that the bank had failed before the checks could be turned in. One of the magazines continued to send us the year's subscription, and someone on the staff of the Literary Guild bought an etching and that paid for the books we had received. The rest were stopped. The stores were not so kind. There were threats to sue, but the justice of the peace, who is also the general store keeper, the game warden and the postmaster, was sympathetic, having lost a few dollars himself in the bank. Later the bank paid a small dividend, and the stores were satisfied.

One day Savannah and I spent the day with old Granny Blair, who taught us to spin thread from cotton and wool, and weave it into cloth, and her husband promised to make me a loom just like hers. But the work was long and tedious, taking days to make a little cotton cloth that could be bought for 5 cents a yard. I often say that I will some day get to it, but I know that I never will, as long as the clothes we have last, and we can continue trading etchings for shoes.

Once a week we walk the twenty miles to and from the post office for our mail. We are still tenderfoot enough to feel the effect of it, for the road is steep and rough. But the thought of the lounging pajamas and slippers that Savannah will have out for us and the warm milk and buttered scones with blackberry jam she will have ready make the climb worth while.

Though we do our own baking and cheesemaking, and plowing and hoeing the garden, we never before had so much leisure. We have also found time to enter into the life of the settlement. Howard has been called upon to act as a lawyer and doctor. Old man Leach had fought in the Civil War, but his widow forgot which side he was on. He would not take a pension during his lifetime. "Not as long as I got two good hands and two laigs will I take nary penny from nobody," he said. But Mrs. Leach did not share his scruples.

"Mr. Howard," she said, "you been around a whole lot and know a lot of people. Can you tell Mr. Hoover to git me that there widow's pension Uncle Mike said I orter be a gittin'?"

Doctor Evans is our only doctor within a radius of thirty miles, and that means mule miles instead of automobile miles. He is an old man, past eighty, and he has had no more than two years' schooling in his life. He obtained his license when the State was young and not so strict, and because we are a poor settlement, and can pay for our health only with calves and pigs and chickens, the town doctors have allowed him to go on practicing. His sole knowledge of medicine is contained in the directions on the patent med-icines he has bought, and his sixty years of experience. He is a conscientious old man, though. He has no home, liv-ing with whichever patient needs him most, often sleeping on a pallet on the kitchen floor. His speciality is gunshot and knife wounds, for he has had much practice in that in our moonshining community. He is never called in on an obstetric case, for that is left to the women folks.

One day last winter, word reached us that little Jewel was sick, and would we go for the doctor. We found him at the Blair place, where old Mrs. Blair was ailing. It was after dark when we reached the sick baby, for we had to go around thirty-five miles by automobile to reach a place six miles from us.

By questioning Ameriky, we learned that the baby's ill-ness had started with a cold, and she was teething at the same time. "I give her some pole cat grease fer her cold, and she perked right up," Ameriky said. And Oval had gone out into the woods and killed a rabbit so that Ameriky could rub the baby's gums with its brains, a remedy every mountain mother uses. Then the child had summer com-plaint, or diarrhea, and was given laudanum, paregoric, whisky, castor oil, black draught, and then more medicine. Everything was given that Ameriky could think of and everything that her neighbors told her about.

When the doctor brought out his ever-present dose of strychnine, and began tearing strips of Sears Roebuck catalog paper to portion out doses from his collection of medicines, Howard grabbed his hat and whispered to me that he was going for the county nurse. It was a long rough ride to the county seat and our tires were worn, but I bade him Godspeed.

We had stood silently by and watched Mrs. Thompson bathe her child sick with chicken pox, in the blood of a freshly killed chicken. And we had seen a young man die of a burst appendix because his wife said she was afeared of hospitals when we offered to take him to one. But our little homestead baby was too close to us to allow to die without trying to save her.

For the first time, I felt our helpfulness in the wilderness and understood the natives' need for a religion of faith. When I made my way through the crowd of men, women and children who had come to set up, I saw little Jewel, lying white and thin on her straw bed, with an old quilt used for a sheet. I quietly reached down and killed a bed bug that was crawling on her arm.

"I jist caint git shet of them thangs," Ameriky told me. "The bats brang them here. They lay the eggs in the walls."

Soon after the dose of strychnine, Jewel began to rally.

"She's a gittin' better. I know she's a goin' to git well," Oval said. "I been a prayin'."

About that time a whippoorwill was heard near the window. This means to the mountain people a message of death, and I shuddered.

"Somebody kill that dratted bird," a woman screamed. "You William, chunk a rock up thar and kill that bird." But William did not succeed, and the bird went on with its innocent call all during the night.

When a screech owl called out in the darkness, an old man quickly turned his overall pocket inside out and wrung it, thus wringing the neck of the owl. The call grew fainter and fainter, finally dying away.

Would Howard never come, I thought. Hours must have gone by. The children were sleeping on pallets around the floor. I was sitting with the grown-ups around the fire, scarcely listening to the tales of death and haints that are always told when people come to set up with the sick. At last I heard two cars in the distance come bumping along the rocky road. I knew Howard had brought the county nurse.

When there is a doctor in attendance, the county nurse is not allowed to express an opinion about a case, but she saw that the child needed immediate attention. We pleaded an hour or so with the doctor and the parents to send the child to a hospital where she would be given every chance to get well. At last they agreed, but it was with reluctance that Oval and Ameriky with the baby in her arms were bundled in the nurse's car at dawn and began their long drive to Little Rock.

But they were too late. It was over a week after little Jewel had been buried and her little grave had been duly decorated with broken bits of colored pottery, that we learned of it.

"You orter seen that place," Ameriky told me two months later when her second baby was born, and she could bring herself to talk about Jewel. "She war in a room with lots of other little children, and they wuz so clean. She had two white sheets put on fresh ever day, and if they even spilt a little water on the bed, they went and changed again. I'm glad we went. She couldn't have got well nohow, but I'm glad she had such a nice place to die in."

* * *

We've spent many pleasant afternoons this summer on some neighbor's porch, with our bare feet resting on the cool floor, discussing the latest gossip, who has been cut or shot in a brawl, or how Miss Marthy's baby was brought into the world by Grandpap Tillar, because we women folks could not reach her in time, and how Miss Marthy will never get over the embarrassment of having a man attend her. And we would hear again of how Dick Bly got on a drunk that lasted a week, and held a revival over at Wild Cat Ridge, and saved five souls. He came to as he walked out into the water to baptize them, and walked away saying, "Hell, I ain't fitten fer this job."

We have so adjusted ourselves to the life of the mountains that we have no actual need for money. The battery of our automobile has long since died, and the tires are worn out by the rocks on the road, so no money need be spent for gasoline. Once a week the peddler comes from the city and trades flour and sugar and salt for chickens, eggs and butter. Savannah has had twenty-five cents in her purse since we gave it to her two months ago, and Howard has been carrying a half dollar around in his pocket so long it is getting rusty.

All along our letters have been full of enthusiasm. We have written glowingly of our freedom from financial worries and our leisure to do whatever we wanted to do. To those friends who bathe in lavender bath tubs with sweet smelling salts, we wrote of bathing in Cove Creek amongst the water-lilies screened by willows, and taking our shower at a tiny waterfall.

Now that the house is completed, the rose garden growing, and the pumpkins, sweet potatoes, peas and corn harvested, we can sit back and say that it has been successful, this experiment of sustaining life on the soil.

But it has really proven nothing except that, whatever the cause of this world economic disturbance, the remedy is not back to the soil, to the simple life of our forefathers, in spite of what the theorists sitting on easy chairs in warm houses may say. We have enjoyed creating Possum Trot, even the hard work, the hunger and the poverty, for that was part of our scheme. But we have learned to our astonishment, that it was the creating we enjoyed. We are still not satisfied. There is a restlessness within us that we cannot defeat, that is as old as mankind. We want more than a roof over our heads and food in our stomachs. Luxuries are as necessary as bread to those of us who have known them. When every drop of water you use is drawn from a seventy-foot well, and every bit of food you eat must be forced from a rocky soil with a hand hoe, you don't feel that machines are your enemies. We want light again by pressing a button, and water, hot or cold, by the turn of a tap, and steam heat and iced lemonade. We are already pricing water systems and electric systems in the mail-order catalogs, and I have been looking longingly at the pictures of kerosene refrigerators and washing machines.

We know that when the depression is over, and people start going around once more with confident faces, buying paintings, etchings and illustrated books, and money comes to us once more, we will not spend it wisely as we once had planned. We will not add to the potato house or build the guest cottage. We'll go back to the city, and once more Howard will wander through the art galleries, or mingle again with friends in his profession. And I can think of nothing I would like more to do than to hand one of those little green papers I have not seen in so long, to a salesgirl, and be given a neatly tied parcel, containing anything, I don't care what, and hear again the clinking of silver change going from her hand to mine, and into my purse. I'd get once more into silk stockings and a chiffon dress and Howard would take his tuxedo from out of the moth ball box, and we'd go to a symphony concert, or we'd hear Fritz Kreisler play his violin. And as on that day when we filed our homestead claim and started cutting down trees for our home, we'd say, "After all, this is really living."

Time Line of Charlie May Simon's Life Events and Book-Length Works

---

1897: Born Charlie May Hogue to Charles Wayman Hogue and Mary Gill Hogue on August 17 near Monticello, Arkansas, in a tenant-farmer log cabin.

1920: Marries Walter Bernard Lowenstein on December 28.

1923: Lowenstein dies, leaving Simon widowed at twenty-six.

1926: Travels to Paris to study art. Meets and marries Howard Simon.

1930 or 1931: Homesteading, and the building of her cabin, begins in Perry Country, Arkansas, during the late spring.

1932: Simon's father publishes *Back Yonder*, his memoir of his youth in the Ozark hills of Arkansas. Laura Ingalls Wilder publishes the first of her *Little House on the Prairie* books.

1933: "Retreat to the Land" appears in the May issue of
Scribner's Magazine.

1934: *Robin on the Mountain* (E. P. Dutton & Co.)

1935: *Lost Corner* (E. P. Dutton & Co.)

1936: Divorces Howard Simon on January 6. Marries John
Gould Fletcher on January 18.

1936: *Teeny Gay* (E. P. Dutton & Co.)

1937: Publishes *The Sharecropper* (E. P. Dutton & Co.), the only
adult-fiction novel she will write.

1938: *Popo's Miracle* (E. P. Dutton & Co.)

1939: *Bright Morning* (E. P. Dutton & Co.)

1940: *Faraway Trail* (E. P. Dutton & Co.)

1940: Homestead cabin destroyed by fire the night before
Simon and Fletcher plan to move into it during construction of their home, Johnswood, outside Little Rock.

1941: *Roundabout* (E. P. Dutton & Co.). Construction of
Johnswood completed in December.

1942: *Lonnie's Landing & Younger Brother* (E. P. Dutton & Co.).
Expenses from taxes and building Johnswood now require
Simon to produce two children's books yearly to cover
debts, doubling her writing deadlines.

1943: *Lays of the New Land: Stories of Some American Poets and Their Work* (E. P. Dutton & Co.)

1943: *Song of Tomorrow* (E. P. Dutton & Co.)

1945: *Straw in the Sun* (E. P. Dutton & Co.)

1945: *Art in the New Land: Stories of Some American Artists and Their Work* (E. P. Dutton & Co.)

1946: *Joe Mason, Apprentice to Audubon* (E. P. Dutton & Co.)

1947: Boys Clubs of America (now Boys & Girls Clubs of America) recognizes *Joe Mason* as the best junior book of 1947.

1948: *The Royal Road* (E. P. Dutton & Co.)

1950: John Gould Fletcher commits suicide on May 10.

1950: *Saturday's Child* (E. P. Dutton & Co.)

1952: *The Long Hunt* (E. P. Dutton & Co.)

1953: *Johnswood* (E. P. Dutton & Co.)

1955: *Secret on the Congo* (Ginn & Company)

1956: *Green Grows the Prairie* (Aladdin)

1956: *All Men Are Brothers: A Portrait of Albert Schweitzer* (E. P. Dutton & Co.)

1958: *A Seed Shall Serve: The Story of Toyohiko Kagawa, Spiritual Leader of Modern Japan* (E. P. Dutton & Co.). Receives the Albert Schweitzer Book Award.

1960: *The Sun and the Birch: The Story of Crown Prince Akihito and Crown Princess Michiko* (E. P. Dutton & Co.)

1960: Receives an honorary doctorate from the University of Arkansas in Fayetteville.

1965: *The Andrew Carnegie Story* (E. P. Dutton & Co.)

1967: *Dag Hammarskjöld* (E. P. Dutton & Co.)

1969: *Martin Buber: Wisdom in Our Time* (E. P. Dutton & Co.)

1970: Receives the Jewish Book Council Award for *Martin Buber*. The Arkansas Department of Education establishes the Charlie May Simon Book Award to honor the author's life and work; the first award is presented the following year.

1972: *Razorbacks Are Really Hogs!* (Garrard & Company)

1974: *Faith Has Need of All the Truth: A Life of Pierre Teilhard de Chardin* (E. P. Dutton & Co.)

1977: Dies March 21 in Little Rock at age 79. Interred at Mount Holly Cemetery beside husband John Gould Fletcher.